debbie bliss
the **baby knits** book

the ultimate collection of
knitwear designs for 0–3 year olds

EBURY PRESS

LONDON

For my very special friend
Patsy and her mother Isabel

First published in Great Britain in 2002

3 5 7 9 10 8 6 4 2

Text © Debbie Bliss 2002
Photographs © Sandra Lousada 2002

First published by Ebury Press
Random House, 20 Vauxhall Bridge Road,
London SW1V 2SA

Random House Australia (Pty) Limited
20 Alfred Street, Milsons Point, Sydney,
New South Wales 2061, Australia

Random House New Zealand Limited
18 Poland Road, Glenfield, Auckland 10,
New Zealand

Random House South Africa (Pty) Limited
Endulini, 5A Jubilee Road, Parktown 2193,
South Africa

The Random House Group Limited
Reg. No. 954009

www.randomhouse.co.uk

A CIP catalogue record for this book is
available from the British Library.

Editor: Sally Harding
Designers: Maggie Town and Beverly Price
Photographer: Sandra Lousada
Stylist: Sammie Bell
Pattern checker: Rosy Tucker
Charts: Anthony Duke

ISBN 0091885132

Colour separation by Colorlito, Milan

Printed and bound in Singapore
by Tien Wah Press

contents

introduction

There is always something very special about knitting for babies and children – nothing can compare to the message and unique quality that hand-knitted garments hold.

The Baby Knits Book is divided into Simple, Cosy and Special. The Simple chapter includes easy knits for the beginner and for those, like new mothers, who do not have much time on their hands. The designs here are worked in basic stitches and classic styles – a soft cashmere-mix jacket and top, a throw, luxurious and gentle enough to wrap against a baby's skin, a kimono and a tank top. The Cosy chapter has generous sweaters to snuggle into, outdoor sporty knits for active children, and a bear in a lamb suit to cuddle up to. In the Special section jackets and shoes are embellished with embroidery and beads, perfect for gifts, and there is an heirloom alphabet blanket to be cherished for years.

All the designs have been knitted in my own range of yarns which have been especially selected not only for their baby-friendly handle but for their easy wash and wear as well. The collection has also been put together to reflect the range of knitting skills, from the basic to the more advanced.

designing for children

There are certain points I always try to keep in mind when I am designing for babies and children. I tend to produce cardigans rather than sweaters for small babies as they dislike having garments pulled over their heads, and it can be difficult to dress them when they are too small to sit up. If I am working on a sweater design for this age I will introduce a shoulder fastening, an envelope neck, or a front or back neck opening. Another practical style is a ballerina, cross-over style which avoids buttons, as they can be uncomfortable when babies roll on to their tummies. I will only use yarn that I know is soft and kind to babies' skin.

Older children can be more of a challenge. I believe that we often have to use all our powers of persuasion to encourage them to wear hand knits. They have been brought up in a world of fleeces, sweatshirts and man-made fibres, and they are used to wearing fabrics that move with them and are light, soft and comfortable. With this thought uppermost, I allow plenty of ease in the garments, especially at the underarm, and particularly if they are worked in a very textured pattern such as an Aran which produces a denser and less elastic fabric.

I always quote the actual measurements of the garments and the age of the wearer rather than the chest measurement. This is because from personal experience although I could always remember the age of my children, I floundered when it came to knowing the chest size! The chest size can also be rather a red herring – all designs, unless they are very tightly fitting fashion garments for an adult, have ease. Ease is the extra measurement allowed for comfort and movement, and also to create a particular style such as a generous outerwear cabled sweater. Some readers have queried the quoted measurements on my children's designs because they are comparing adult's chest measurements with the actual measurements of a child's garment. I usually ask them to measure an existing garment that the child they are knitting for wears, and they are usually surprised to find that they match up closely to the measurements in the pattern. I also like to think that the time and money, not to mention love, that has been invested into knitting the design should be rewarded by having a knit that will see the child through at least a couple of years, even if a rather larger than is strictly needed garment is produced originally. However, if the reader is not happy with my measurements I will always suggest that they knit a smaller or larger size.

Try to involve the child in the design you are knitting for them rather than just produce one in the colours or style you like! It is a wonderful opportunity to teach them from an early age that not all their clothes just appear by magic in shops, that they can be lovingly made especially for them. It is also a great way to introduce them to the craft and to looking at colours and textures. Even choosing buttons can be fun.

Debbie Bliss

basic information

Following pattern instructions

Figures for larger sizes are given in round ( ) brackets. Where only one figure appears, this applies to all sizes. Work the figures given in square [ ] brackets the number of times stated afterwards. Where 0 appears, no stitches or rows are worked for this size. As you follow the pattern, make sure that you are consistently using the right stitches for your size – it is only too easy to switch sizes inside the brackets. One way to avoid this is to go through the instructions first and mark off the size you are knitting with a coloured marker or highlighter.

The quantities of yarn quoted in the instructions are based on the yarn used by the knitter for the original garment and amounts should therefore be considered approximate. A slight variation in tension can make the difference between using less or more yarn than that stated in the pattern. Before buying the yarn look at the measurements in the knitting patterns to be sure which size you want to knit. My patterns quote the actual finished size of the garment, not the chest size of the wearer. The length of the garment is taken from the shoulder shaping to the cast-on edge.

Tension

Each pattern in the book states a tension or gauge – the number of stitches and rows per centimetre or inch that should be obtained with the given needles, yarn and stitch pattern. Check your tension carefully before starting work. A slight variation in tension can spoil the look of a garment and alter the proportions that the designer wanted. A too loose tension will produce uneven knitting and an unstable fabric that can droop or lose it's shape after washing, whilst too tight a tension can create a hard, unforgiving fabric.

To make a tension square use the same needles, yarn and stitch pattern quoted in the tension note in the pattern. Knit a sample at least 12.5cm/5in square. Smooth out the finished sample on a flat surface but do not stretch it. To check the stitch tension place a tape measure horizontally on the sample and mark 10cm/4in with pins. Count the number of

stitches between pins. To check the row tension place the tape measure vertically on the sample and mark 10cm/4in. Count the number of rows between the pins. If the number of stitches and rows is greater than that stated in the pattern, try again using larger needles. If the number of stitches and rows is less, use smaller needles. If you are only able to obtain either the stitch or the row tension, it is the stitch tension that is the most important to get right, as the length of many patterns are calculated by measurement rather than the amount or rows you need to work to achieve it.

Garment care

Taking care of your knitted garments is important. If you have invested all that time and labour into knitting them, you want them to look good for as long as possible. Follow these guidelines for the best results.

Check the yarn label for washing instructions. Most yarns can now be machine washed on a delicate wool cycle. Prior to washing, make a note of the measurements of the garment, such as the width and length. After washing, lay the garment flat and check the measurements again to see if they are the same. If not, smooth and pat it back into shape.

Some knitters prefer to hand wash their garments. Use soap flakes specially created for hand knits, and warm rather

Needle conversion chart

This needle conversion chart covers all the knitting needle sizes used for the patterns in this book.

UK metric	US sizes
2¾mm	size 2
3mm	size 2/3
3¼mm	size 3
3¾mm	size 5
4mm	size 6
4½mm	size 7
5mm	size 8

UK and US knitting terminology

The following terms that are used in the book may be unfamiliar to US readers.

UK term	US term
Aran wool	'fisherman' yarn
ball band	yarn wrapper or label
brackets, round	parentheses
brackets, square	brackets
cast off	bind off
double knitting	a yarn weight between sport and worsted
every alternate row	every other row
make up	finish
moss stitch	seed stitch
plait	braid
stocking stitch	stockinette stitch
tension	gauge
yf	yarn over (yo), or yarn to front of work between two needles
yon, yrn	yarn over (yo)

Standard abbreviations

alt = alternate
beg = begin(ning)
cont = continu(e)ing
dec = decreas(e)ing
foll = following
inc = increas(e)ing
k = knit
m1 = make one by picking up the loop lying between st just worked and next st and working into back of it
patt = pattern
p = purl
psso = pass slipped st over
rem = remain(ing)
rep = repeat(ing)
skpo = slip 1, knit 1, pass slipped stitch over
sl = slip
st(s) = stitch(es)
st st = stocking stitch
tbl = through back loop
tog = together
yf = yarn forward
yon = yarn over needle
yrn = yarn round needle

than hot water. Handle the knits gently in the water – do not rub or wring, as this can felt the fabric. Rinse well to get rid of any soap, and squeeze out excess water. You may need to get rid of more water by rolling the garment in a towel, or you can use the delicate spin cycle of the washing machine. Dry the garment by laying it out flat on top of a towel to absorb moisture, smooth and pat into shape. Do not dry knits near direct heat such as a radiator. Store your knits loosely folded to allow the air to circulate.

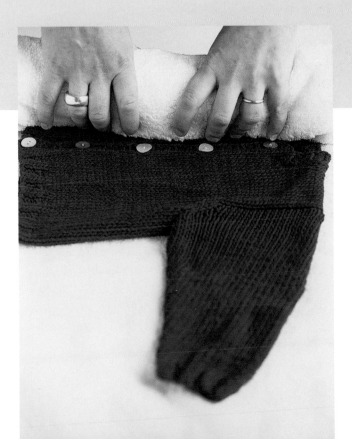

types of yarns

Fibres are divided into two main categories, natural and synthetic. Natural fibres are then divided into animal fibres – wool, angora, cashmere, silk, etc. – and those from vegetable fibres such as cotton, linen and hemp. This is a guide to the yarns used in this book.

Wool

Wool spun from the fleece of sheep is the yarn that is the most commonly associated with knitting. It has many excellent qualities, as it is durable, elastic, and warm in the winter. Wool yarn is particularly good for working colour patterns, as the fibres adhere together and help prevent the gaps that can appear in Fair Isle or intarsia.

Some knitters find that a simple stitch such as moss stitch or garter stitch can look neater when worked in a wool rather than a cotton yarn.

Cotton

Cotton yarn, made from a natural plant fibre, is an ideal all-seasons yarn, as it is warm in the winter and cool in the summer. I particularly love to work in cotton because it gives a clarity of stitch that shows up subtle stitch patterning such as a moss stitch border on a collar or cuffs.

Cotton and wool

Knitting in yarn that is a blend of wool and cotton is particularly good for children's wear. This is because the wool fibres give elasticity for comfort and the cotton content is perfect for children who find wool irritating against the skin.

Cashmere

Cashmere is made from the underhair of a particular Asian goat. It is associated with the ultimate in luxury, and is unbelievably soft to the touch. If combined with merino wool and microfibre, as in my cashmerino yarn range, it is perfect for babies.

Silk

Silk is a fibre produced by certain caterpillars as they spin their cocoon. Combined with cotton, as in my cotton/silk range, it can make beautiful yarn that also has hardwearing qualities.

buying yarn

Always try to buy the yarn quoted in the knitting pattern. The designer will have created the design specifically with that yarn in mind and a substitute may produce a garment that is different from the original. For instance, the design may rely for it's appeal on a subtle stitch pattern that is lost when using a yarn of an inferior quality, or a synthetic when used to replace a natural yarn such as cotton will create a limp fabric and the crispness of the original design lost. We cannot accept responsibility for the finished product if any yarn other than the one specified is used.

If you do decide to use a substitute yarn buy a yarn that is the same weight and where possible the same fibre content. It is essential to use a yarn that has the same tension as the original or the measurements will change. You should also check metreage or yardage – yarn that weighs the same may have different lengths so you may need to buy more or less yarn. Check the ball band on the yarn. Most yarn labels now carry all the information you need about fibre content, washing instructions, weight and metreage or yardage.

It is essential to check the dye lot number on the yarn label. Yarns are dyed in batches or lots, which can sometimes vary quite considerably. Your retailer may not have the same dye lot later on, so try and buy all your yarn for a project at the same time. If you know that sometimes you use more yarn than that quoted in the pattern, buy more. If it is not possible to buy the amount you need all in the same dye lot, work the borders or the lower edges in the odd one since the colour change is less likely to show here.

debbie bliss yarns

The following are descriptions of my yarns and a guide to their weights and types. All the yarns used in the designs are machine washable. (See page 128 for yarn distributors.)

Debbie Bliss merino double knitting: a 100% merino wool in a double-knitting weight. Soft to the touch but hardwearing. Approximately 110m/50g ball.

Debbie Bliss merino aran: a 100% merino wool in an Aran or fisherman weight. Ideal for outerwear. Approximately 78m/50g ball.

Debbie Bliss wool/cotton: a 50% merino wool, 50% cotton lightweight yarn that is between a 4-ply and a double knitting. This yarn combines the crispness of cotton with the elasticity of wool. Approximately 107m/50g ball.

Debbie Bliss cashmerino aran: a 55% merino wool, 33% microfibre, 12% cashmere yarn in an Aran or fisherman weight. A luxurious yarn with a beautiful handle. Approximately 90m/50g ball.

Debbie Bliss baby cashmerino: a 55% merino wool, 33% microfibre, 12% cashmere lightweight yarn between a 4-ply and a double knitting. It is perfect for knitting for newborn and small babies as it is gentle against the skin. Approximately 125m/50g ball.

Debbie Bliss cotton double knitting: a 100% cotton yarn in a double-knitting weight. It knits up smoothly, showing up stitch detail well. Approximately 84m/50g ball.

Debbie Bliss cotton/silk: a 80% cotton, 20% silk yarn in an Aran weight. It has the crispness of cotton with a slight sheen. Approximately 63m/50g ball.

simple

coathanger

The easiest of makes, this moss stitch coathanger has a contrasting edge and is trimmed with a pretty bow. It is a great first project for a beginner.

Materials

One 50g ball of Debbie Bliss cotton double knitting in Main shade (M) and small amount in Contrast shade (C).
Pair of 4mm(US 6) knitting needles.
Small amount of wadding.
30cm/12in wooden coathanger.
30cm/12in narrow ribbon.

Tension

20 sts and 30 rows to 10cm/4in over moss st using 4mm(US 6) needles.

Abbreviations See page 7.

To make

With 4mm(US 6) needles and C, cast on 61 sts.
K 4 rows.
Change to M.
K 1 row.
Next row K1, * p1, k1; rep from * to end.
This row forms moss st.
Cont in moss st until work measures 11cm/4½in from beg, ending with a right side row.
K 1 row.
Change to C.
K 4 rows.
Cast off.

To make up

Lightly pad the hanger with wadding. Place knitting around the hanger and stitch cast on and cast off edges together. Sew up side seams. Tie ribbon in a bow around hanger neck.

moss stitch hat, scarf and throw

Knitted in reversible moss stitch and worked in a cashmere mix, the hat and scarf are an ideal gift set for a new knitter to make for a new baby. The baby blanket is a perfect size for a small pram or buggy.

Measurements
Hat and scarf:
To fit ages   3-6 months
Scarf length   59cm/23in
Scarf width   11cm/4¼in
Throw:
Approximately 56 x 74cm/22 x 29in.

Materials
Hat: One 50g ball of Debbie Bliss cashmerino aran in Main shade (M) and small amount in Contrast shade (C). Pair of 5mm(US 8) knitting needles.
Scarf: Two 50g balls of Debbie Bliss cashmerino aran in Main shade (M) and small amount in Contrast shade (C). Pair each of 4½mm(US 7) and 5mm (US 8) knitting needles.
Throw: Six 50g balls of Debbie Bliss cashmerino aran in Main shade (M) and two balls in Contrast shade (C). Pair each of 4½mm(US 7) and 5mm US 8) knitting needles.

Tension
20 sts and 36 rows to 10cm/4in square over moss st using 5mm(US 8) needles.

Abbreviations See page 7.

Note When changing colours on Throw, twist yarns together on the wrong side to avoid holes.

Hat
With 5mm(US 8) needles and C, cast on 72 sts.
Beg with a k row, work 5 rows in st st.
Change to M.
P 1 row.
1st row [K1, p1] to end.
2nd row [P1, k1] to end.
These 2 rows form moss st.
Cont in moss st until work measures 13cm/5in from cast on edge, ending with a wrong side row.
Shape top
Next row [Moss st 6, work 3tog] to end. 56 sts.
Work 3 rows.
Next row [Moss st 4, work 3tog] to end. 40 sts.
Work 3 rows.
Next row [Moss st 2, work 3tog] to end. 24 sts.
Work 1 row.
Next row [Work 3tog] to end. 8 sts.
Break yarn, leaving a long end. Thread through rem sts, pull up and secure. Join seam, reversing seam on contrast roll.

Scarf
With 4½mm(US 7) needles and C, cast on 21 sts.
K 4 rows.
Change to 5mm(US 8) needles and M.
K 1 row.
Next row K3, * p1, k1; rep from * to last 4 sts, p1, k3.
Rep the last row until work measures 58cm/23in from cast on edge, ending with a wrong side row.

Change to 4½mm(US 7) needles and C.

K 4 rows.

Cast off.

Throw

With 4½mm(US 7) and C, cast on 113 sts.

K 4 rows.

Change to 5mm(US 8) needles.

Next row K3C, k with M to last 3 sts, k3C.

Next row K3C, * k1M, p1M; rep from * to last 4 sts, k1M, k3C.

Rep the last row, working moss st in M with k3C at each end of every row, until work measures 72cm/28in, ending with a wrong side row.

Next row With C, k to end.

Change to 4½mm(US 7) needles.

K 4 rows in C.

Cast off.

tank top

Knitted in stocking stitch with a wool and cotton mix, this sleeveless summer top is a stylish alternative to the classic T-shirt.

Measurements

To fit ages

3-6	6-9	9-12	12-24	24-36	mths

Actual measurements

Chest

45	49	53	58	63	cm
17¾	19¼	21	22¾	24¾	in

Length to shoulder

22	24	26	30	34	cm
8¾	9½	10¼	11¾	13½	in

Materials

2(2:3:3:3) 50g balls of Debbie Bliss wool/cotton.
Pair each of 3mm(US 2) and 3¼mm (US 3) knitting needles.

Tension

25 sts and 34 rows to 10cm/4in square over st st using 3¼mm(US 3) needles.

Abbreviations See page 7.

Back

With 3mm(US 2) needles cast on 58(64:68:74:80) sts.
Rib row * K1, p1; rep from * to end.
Rep the rib row 3(3:5:5:7) times more.
Change to 3¼mm(US 3) needles.
Beg with a k row, work in st st until back measures 12(13:14:17:20)cm/4¾(5:5½:6¾:8)in from cast on edge, ending with a p row.

Shape armholes
Cast off 3(4:4:5:5) sts at beg of next 2 rows.
Dec one st at each end of the next and 3(3:4:4:5) foll alt rows. 44(48:50:54:58) sts.
Cont in st st until back measures 20(22:24:28:32)cm/8(8¾:9½:11:12½)in from cast on edge, ending with a p row.

Shape neck
Next row K15(16:17:18:19) sts, turn and work on these sts for first side of back neck.
Dec one st at neck edge on next 4 rows. 11(12:13:14:15) sts.
Work 3 rows. Cast off.
With right side facing, slip centre 14(16:16:18:20) sts onto a holder, rejoin yarn to rem sts, k to end.
Complete to match first side of neck shaping.

Front

Work as given for Back until front measures 16(18:20:23:27)cm/6¼(7:8:9:10½)in from cast on edge, ending with a p row.

Shape neck
Next row K17(18:19:20:21) sts, turn and work on these sts for first side of front neck.

Dec one st at neck edge on next and every foll alt row until 11(12:13:14:15) sts rem.

Work straight until front measures same as Back to shoulder, ending with a p row.

Cast off.

With right side facing, slip centre 10(12:12:14:16) sts onto a holder, rejoin yarn to rem sts, k to end.

Complete to match first side of neck shaping.

Neckband

Join right shoulder seam.

With right side facing and 3mm(US 2) needles, pick up and k20(20:20:22:22) sts down left side of front neck, k across 10(12:12:14:16) sts from front neck holder, pick up and k20(20:20:22:22) sts up right side of front neck, 10 sts down right back neck, k across 14(16:16:18:20) sts from back neck holder, pick up and k10 sts up left back neck. 84(88:88:96:100) sts.

Work 4(4:4:6:6) rows in rib as given for Back.

Cast off in rib.

Armbands

Join left shoulder and neckband seam.

With right side facing and 3mm(US 2) needles, pick up and k60(68:72:80:86) sts around armhole edge.

Work 4(4:4:6:6) rows in rib as given for Back.

Cast off in rib.

To make up

Join side and armband seams.

double-breasted jacket and leggings

Measurements
Jacket: To fit ages

3-6	6-12	12-18	18-24	mths

Actual measurements

Chest

60	65	70	75	cm
23½	25½	27½	29½	in

Length

26	30	35	39	cm
10¼	11¾	13¾	15¼	in

Sleeve seam (with cuff turned back)

14	18	20	22	cm
5½	7	8	8½	in

Leggings:

To fit ages	3-6	6-12	mths

Actual measurements

Width	54	64	cm
	21¼	25½	in
Length	29	37	cm
	11½	14½	in
Inside leg seam	12	17	cm
	4¾	6¾	in

Materials
Jacket: 5(6:7:8) 50g balls Debbie Bliss wool/cotton. Pair each of 2¾mm(US 2) and 3¼mm(US 3) knitting needles. 6(8:10:10) buttons.

Leggings: 3(3) 50g balls of Debbie Bliss wool/cotton. Pair each of 2¾mm(US 2) and 3¼mm(US 3) knitting needles. Waist length of 1cm/½in wide elastic.

Tension
25 sts and 34 rows to 10cm/4in square over st st using 3¼mm(US 3) needles.

Abbreviations See page 7.

This smart outfit has been designed in the style of a 1950's pram set. The jacket has a double-breasted fastening and a half belt at the back. This is for the busy rather than the new knitter.

JACKET
Back
With 3¼mm(US 3) needles cast on 75(81:87:93) sts.

Moss st row K1, * p1, k1; rep from * to end.

Rep this row 4(4:4:6) times more.

Beg with a k row, work in st st until back measures 26(30:35:39)cm/10¼(11¾:13¾:15¼)in from cast on edge, ending with a p row.

Shape shoulders

Cast off 13(14:15:16) sts at beg of next 4 rows.

Cast off rem 23(25:27:29) sts.

Pocket Linings (make 2)
With 3¼mm(US 3) needles cast on 17(19:23:23) sts.

Beg with a k row, work 20 rows in st st.

Leave sts on a holder.

Right Front
With 3¼mm(US 3) needles cast on 49(53:57:59) sts.

Work 5(5:5:7) rows in moss st as given for Back.

Next row (right side) Moss st 21(23:25:27), k to end.

Next row P28(30:32:32), moss st to end.

These two rows set the position of the st st with moss st front panel.

Work a further 26(28:28:30) rows.

Place pocket
Next row (right side) Moss st 21(23:25:27), k1, slip next 17(19:23:23) sts onto a holder, k across 17(19:23:23) sts of first pocket lining, k to end.

Work 13(5:7:1) rows.

** **1st buttonhole row** (right side) Moss st 3, cast off 2, moss st next 9(11:13:15), cast off 2, moss st next 3, k to end.

2nd buttonhole row P28(30:32:32), moss st 4, cast on 2, moss st 10(12:14:16), cast on 2, moss st 3.

Work 26(20:26:20) rows. **

Rep from ** to ** 0(1:1:2) times more.

2nd, 3rd and 4th sizes only

1st buttonhole row (right side) Moss st 3, cast off 2, moss st next (11:13:15), cast off 2, moss st next 3, k to end.

2nd buttonhole row P(30:32:32), moss st 4, cast on 2, moss st (12:14:16), cast on 2, moss st 3.

All sizes

Work 2 rows, so ending with a wrong side row.

Shape neck

Next row Cast off 18 sts in moss st, patt to end.

Dec one st at neck edge of next 5(7:9:9) rows. 26(28:30:32) sts.

Work straight until right front matches Back to shoulder, ending at side edge.

Shape shoulder

Next row Cast off 13(14:15:16) sts.

Work 1 row. Cast off rem 13(14:15:16) sts.

Left Front

Work as given for Right Front, omitting buttonholes, reversing shapings and placing pocket as follows:

Next row (right side) K10(10:8:8), slip next 17(19:23:23) sts onto a holder, k across 17(19:23:23) sts of second pocket lining, k1, moss st 21(23:25:27).

Sleeves

With 3¼mm(US 3) needles cast on 37(39:43:45) sts.

Work 21 rows in moss st as given for Right Front.

Change to 2¾mm(US 2) needles and work a further 21 rows in moss st.

Change to 3¼mm(US 3) needles.

Beg with a k row, work in st st.

Inc one st at each end of 3rd and every foll 5th row until there are 47(51:61:67) sts.

Cont straight until sleeve measures 19(23:25:27)cm/ 7½(9:10:10¼)in from cast on edge. Cast off.

Collar

Join shoulder seams.

With right side facing, 2¾mm(US 2) needles and beg 11 sts in from right front edge, pick up and k23(24:26:28) sts up right front neck to shoulder, 29(31:33:35) sts across back neck, 23(24:26:28) sts down left front neck, ending 11 sts in from left front edge. 75(79:85:91) sts.

Work 1 row in moss st as given for Right Front.

Next 2 rows Moss st to last 23 sts, turn.

Next 2 rows Moss st to last 19 sts, turn.

Next 2 rows Moss st to last 15 sts, turn.

Next 2 rows Moss st to last 11 sts, turn.

Next row Moss st to end.

Moss st 5 rows across all sts.

Change to 3¼mm(US 3) needles.

Moss st 12 rows.

Cast off in moss st.

Back Belt

With 3¼mm(US 3) needles cast on 53(59:65:71) sts.

Work 9 rows in moss st as given for Back.

Cast off in moss st.

Pocket Tops

With right side facing, slip 17(19:23:23) sts from first pocket holder onto 2¾mm(US 2) needles. Work 5 rows in moss st as given for Back.

Cast off in moss st.

Repeat for second pocket.

To make up

Catch down pocket linings and pocket top edges. Sew on sleeves, placing centre of top edge of sleeve to shoulder

seam. Join side and sleeve seams, reversing seam on lower half of cuffs. Turn back cuffs. Sew on buttons. Place belt at desired position on back and secure in place with buttons.

LEGGINGS
Left Leg
With 2¾mm(US 2) needles cast on 69(83) sts.
Beg with a k row, work 3cm/1¼in in st st, ending with a p row.
K 3 rows.
Beg with a p row, cont in st st until work measures 20(23)cm/7¾(9)in from cast on edge, ending with a p row
Shape inside leg
Dec one st at each end of next and every foll 3rd(4th) row until 49(59) sts rem.
Cont straight until work measures 10(15)cm/4(6)in from beg of leg shaping, ending with a p row.
Moss st row K1, * p1, k1; rep from * to end.
Rep this row 5 times more.
Cast off in moss st.

Right Leg
Work exactly as Left Leg.

To make up
Join centre back and front seams. Join inside leg seams. Fold top edge over onto wrong side along ridge row to form a hem and slip stitch in place, leaving an opening in the seam. Thread elastic through hem, stitch ends together, then stitch seam opening closed.

garter stitch jacket and hat

This simple knit is worked all in one, and has neat, turned-back cuffs. Both hat and jacket are worked in garter stitch, which is the easiest stitch of all.

Measurements

Jacket:

To fit ages	3-6	6-9	9-12	mths
Actual measurements				
Chest	56	61	66	cm
	22	24	26	in
Length to shoulder				
	26	28	30	cm
	10¼	11	11¾	in

Sleeve length (with cuff turned back)

	6	18	20	cm
	6¼	7	8	in

Hat:

To fit ages	3-6	6-12 months

Materials

Jacket: 4(5:6) 50g balls of Debbie Bliss cashmerino aran. Pair of 5mm(US 8) knitting needles. 4 buttons.

Hat: 1(2) 50g balls of Debbie Bliss cashmerino aran. Pair of 5mm(US 8) knitting needles.

Tension

18 sts and 36 rows to 10cm/4in square over garter st (k every row) using 5mm(US 8) needles.

Abbreviations See page 7.

JACKET

Worked all in one piece.

With 5mm(US 8) needles cast on 52(57:62) sts.

K 55(59:63) rows.

Shape sleeves

Cast on 6(7:8) sts at beg of next 6 rows and 18(20:22) sts at beg of foll 2 rows. 124(139:154) sts.

K 32(36:40) rows.

Divide for Fronts

Next row K51(58:65) sts, cast off next 22(23:24) sts, k to end.

Cont on last set of 51(58:65) sts for left front.

K 7(9:11) rows.

Shape neck

Inc one st at neck edge on next 6 rows.

Cast on 8 sts at beg of next row. 65(72:79) sts.

K 18(20:22) rows.

Shape sleeve

Cast off 18(20:22) sts at beg of next row and 6(7:8) sts at beg of 3 foll alt rows. 29(31:33) sts.

K 28(32:36) rows.

Make pocket opening

Next row K6(7:8), k next 17 sts and slip these sts onto a holder, k rem 6(7:8) sts.

Next row K6(7:8), cast on 17 sts, k rem 6(7:8) sts.

K 25 rows.

Cast off.

Right Front

With wrong side facing, join yarn to rem sts, k to end.

K 7(9:11) rows.

Shape neck

Inc one st at neck edge on next 6 rows.

Cast on 8 sts at beg of next row.

K 4 rows.

Buttonhole row K to last 4 sts, yf, k2tog, k2.

K11(13:15) rows.

Shape sleeve

Cast off 18(20:22) sts at beg of next row and 6(7:8) sts at beg of 3 foll alt rows. 29(31:33) sts.

K 3 rows.

Buttonhole row K to last 4 sts, yf, k2tog, k2.

K21(23:25) rows.

Buttonhole row K to last 4 sts, yf, k2tog, k2.

K3(5:7) rows.

Make pocket opening

Next row K6(7:8), k next 17 sts and slip these sts onto a holder, k rem 6(7:8) sts.

Next row K6(7:8), cast on 17 sts , k rem 6(7:8) sts.

K 16 rows.

Buttonhole row K to last 4 sts, yf, k2tog, k2.

K 8 rows. Cast off.

Pocket Linings (both alike)

With wrong side facing, slip sts from holder onto a 5mm (US 8) needle, join on yarn.

K 24 rows. Cast off.

To make up

Join side and sleeve seams, reversing seam on cuff for 6cm/2¼in. Sew down pocket linings. Sew on buttons. Turn back cuffs.

HAT

With 5mm(US 8) needles cast on 64(71) sts.

Beg with a k row, work 8 rows in st st.

Cont in garter st until hat measures 13(15)cm/5(6)in from cast on edge.

Shape top

1st dec row K1, [k2tog, k5] 9(10) times. 55(61) sts.

K 3 rows.

2nd dec row K1, [k2tog, k4] 9(10) times. 46(51) sts.

K 3 rows.

Cont to dec in this way on next and foll 2 alt rows. 19(21) sts.

Next row K1, [k2tog] to end. 10(11) sts.

Break yarn, thread through rem sts, pull up and secure. Join seam.

kimono and trousers

This relaxed, wrapover-style kimono has a tie belt and matching trousers. Worked in stocking stitch with garter stitch borders, the set is a simple rather than an easy knit.

Measurements

Kimono: To fit ages

3-6	6-12	12-18	months

Actual measurements

Chest

54	58	62	cm
21¼	22¾	24½	in

Length to shoulder

32	34	36	cm
12½	13½	14¼	in

Sleeve length

16	18	20	cm
6¼	7	8	in

Trousers: To fit ages

3-6	6-12	12-18	months

Actual measurements

Width

52	56	60	cm
20½	22	23½	in

Length

25	30	37	cm
9¾	11¾	14½	in

Inside leg seam

8	11	14	cm
3¼	4¼	5½	in

Materials

Kimono:
3(3:4) 50g balls of Debbie Bliss wool/cotton in Main shade (M) and one 50g ball in Contrast shade (C). Pair each of 3mm(US 2) and 3¼mm (US 3) knitting needles.

Trousers:
3(3:3) 50g balls of Debbie Bliss wool/cotton in Main shade (M) and one 50g ball in Contrast shade (C). Pair each of 3mm(US 2) and 3¼mm (US 3) knitting needles.
Waist length of 1cm/½in wide elastic.

Tension

25 sts and 34 rows to 10cm/4in square over st st using 3¼mm(US 3) needles.

Abbreviations See page 7.

KIMONO

Back

With 3mm(US 2) needles and C, cast on 80(85:90) sts.

K 5 rows.

Change to 3¼mm(US 3) needles and M.

Beg with a k row, work 10(12:14) rows in st st.

Dec row K8, skpo, k to last 10 sts, k2tog, k8.

Cont in st st, work 9 rows.

Rep the last 10 rows 3 times more and the dec row once again. 70(75:80) sts.

Cont straight until back measures 21(22:23)cm/8¼(8¾:9)in from cast on edge, ending with a p row.

Shape armholes

Cast off 6 sts at beg of next 2 rows. 58(63:68) sts.

Cont straight until back measures 32(34:36)cm/12½(13½:14¼)in from cast on edge, ending with a p row.

Shape shoulders

Cast off 7(8:9) sts at beg of next 4 rows.

Leave rem 30(31:32) sts on a holder.

Left Front

With 3mm(US 2) needles and C, cast on 60(63:66) sts.

K 5 rows.

Change to 3¼mm(US 3) needles and M.

Beg with a k row, work 10(12:14) rows in st st.

Dec row (right side) K8, skpo, k to end.

Cont in st st, work 9 rows.

Rep the last 10 rows 3 times more and the dec row once again. 55(58:61) sts.

Work 2 rows, so ending with a k row.

Shape neck

Next row Cast off 7(8:9) sts, p to end. K 1 row.

Next row Cast off 5 sts, p to end. K 1 row.

Next row Cast off 4 sts, p to end.

Next row K to last 2 sts, k2tog.

Cont to dec one st at neck edge on every foll alt row until front measures same as Back to armhole shaping, ending with a p row.

Next row Cast off 6 sts, k to last 2 sts, k2tog.

Keeping armhole edge straight, cont to dec at neck edge on every alt row until 14(16:18) sts rem.

Cont straight until front measures same as Back to shoulder, ending at armhole edge.

Shape shoulder

Cast off 7(8:9) sts at beg of next row.

P 1 row.

Cast off rem 7(8:9) sts.

Right Front

With 3mm(US 2) needles and C, cast on 60(63:66) sts.

K 5 rows.

Change to 3¼mm(US 3) needles and M.

Beg with a k row, work 10(12:14) rows in st st.

Dec row K to last 10 sts, k2tog, k8.

Cont in st st, work 9 rows.

Rep the last 10 rows 3 times more and the dec row once again. 55(58:61) sts.

P 1 row.

Shape neck

Cast off 7(8:9) sts at beg of next row. P 1 row.

Cast off 5 sts at beg of next row. P 1 row.

Cast off 4 sts at beg of next row.

P 1 row.

Next row K2tog, k to end.

Cont to dec one st at neck edge on every foll alt row until front measures same as Back to armhole shaping, ending with a k row.

Next row Cast off 6 sts, p to end.

Keeping armhole edge straight, cont to dec at neck edge on every alt row until 14(16:18) sts rem.

Cont straight until front measures same as Back to shoulder, ending at armhole edge.

Shape shoulder

Cast off 7(8:9) sts at beg of next row.

K 1 row.

Cast off rem 7(8:9) sts.

Sleeves

With 3mm(US 2) needles and C, cast on 40(43:46) sts.
K 5 rows. Change to 3¼mm(US 3) needles and M.
Beg with a k row, work in st st, inc one st at each end of the 3rd and every foll 6th row until there are 54(59:66) sts.
Cont straight until sleeve measures 16(18:20)cm/6¼(7:7¾)in from cast on edge, mark each end of last row, then work a further 2cm/¾in, ending with a p row. Cast off.

Right Front Edging

With right side facing, 3mm(US 2) needles and C, pick up and k43(46:48) sts evenly along right front edge, from cast on edge to start of neck shaping. K 6 rows. Cast off.

Left Front Edging

With right side facing, 3mm(US 2) needles and C, pick up and k43(46:48) sts evenly along left front edge from start of neck shaping to cast on edge. K 6 rows. Cast off.

Neckband

Join shoulder seams.
With right side facing, 3mm(US 2) needles and C, pick up and k3 sts across row ends of right front band, 56(61:66) sts up right front neck, k across 30(31:32) sts at back neck, pick up and k56(61:66) sts down left front neck and 3 sts across row ends of left front band. 148(162:170) sts.
K 6 rows. Cast off.

Ties (make 2)

With 3mm(US 2) needles and C, cast on 6 sts.
Work in garter st until tie measures 43(46:48)cm/17(18:19)in from cast on edge. Cast off.

To make up

Sew on sleeves, sewing last 2cm/¾in above markers to sts cast off at underarm. Sew one tie to each end of neckband. Join side and sleeve seams, leaving an opening in right side seam, level with beg of neck shaping.

TROUSERS

Back and Front (both alike)

With 3mm(US 2) needles and M, cast on 66(72:78) sts.
Rib row * K1, p1; rep from * to end.
Rep the last row 9 times more.
Change to 3¼mm(US 3) needles. Beg with a k row, work in st st until work measures 17(19:23)cm/6¾(7½:9)in from cast on edge, ending with a p row.
Divide for legs
Next row K30(33:36) sts, turn and work on these sts for first leg.
P 1 row.
Dec one st at inside edge of next and 4(5:6) foll alt rows. 25(27:29) sts.
Cont straight until work measures 24(29:36)cm/9½(11½:14¼)in from cast on edge, ending with a p row.
Change to 3mm(US 2) needles and C. K 6 rows. Cast off.
With right side facing and M, rejoin yarn to rem sts, cast off 6 sts, k to end. Complete to match first leg.

To make up

Join side and inside leg seams. Join elastic into a ring. Work a herringbone casing over wrong side of rib at waist, enclosing elastic.

pompon slippers

These slippers are knitted in garter stitch and are free of complicated shaping. For other decorative ideas, turn to page 124.

Measurements
To fit ages 6-12 12-18 months

Materials
One 50g ball of Debbie Bliss wool/cotton in Main shade (M) and small amount in Contrast shade (C). Pair of 2¾mm(US 2) knitting needles.

Tension
28 sts and 60 rows to 10cm/4in square over garter st (k every row) using 2¾mm(US 2) needles.

Abbreviations See page 7.

Note For safety reasons, make sure pompons are sewn on securely.

To make
With 2¾mm(US 2) needles and M, cast on 22(26) sts.
K 1 row.
Work in garter st and inc one st at each end of next and every foll alt row until there are 38(44) sts.
Dec one st at each end of next and every foll alt row until 22(26) sts rem.

Shape heel
Next row Cast on 8(9) sts, k these 8(9) sts, then k to end. 30(35) sts.
K 1 row.
Inc one st at end of next and 6(7) foll alt rows. 37(43) sts.
K 1 row.
Next row Cast off 20(22) sts, k to last st, inc in last st. 18(22) sts.
K 18(22) rows.
Next row K2tog, k to end.
Next row Cast on 20(22) sts, k these 20(22) sts, k to end. 37(43) sts.
Dec one st at beg of next and 6(7) foll alt rows. 30(35) sts.
K 1 row.
Cast off.

To make up
Join back heel seam. Join upper to sole all around, easing in fullness at toes. Turn through to right side. With C, make two small pompons and attach to top of slippers.

raglan sweater

Beautifully simple, this sweater has soft, rolling edges and fully fashioned detailing on the raglan shaping. The cashmere content of the yarn makes it soft against a baby's skin.

Measurements

To fit ages

0-3	3-6	6-9	9-12	mths

Actual measurements

Chest

48	52	56	61	cm
19	20½	22	24	in

Length to shoulder

22	24	26	28	cm
8¾	9½	10¼	11	in

Sleeve length

14	16	18	20	cm
5½	6¼	7	8	in

Materials

3(3:4:4) 50g balls of Debbie Bliss cashmerino aran.
Pair of 5mm(US 8) knitting needles.

Tension

18 sts and 24 rows to 10cm/4in square over st st using 5mm(No 8) needles.

Abbreviations See page 7.

Back and Front (both alike)

With 5mm(US 8) needles, cast on 45(49:53:57) sts.
Beg with a k row, work in st st until work measures 11(12:13:14)cm/4¼(4¾:5:5½)in from cast on edge, ending with a p row.

Shape raglan

Cast off 3 sts at beg of next 2 rows.
1st row K2, skpo, k to last 4 sts, k2tog, k2.
2nd row P to end.
Rep the last 2 rows until 19(21:23:25) sts rem, ending with a p row. Beg with a k row, work 2 rows st st.
Cast off.

Sleeves

With 5mm(US 8) needles cast on 30(32:34:36) sts.
Beg with a k row, work 6 rows st st.
Inc row (right side) K3, m1, k to last 3 sts, m1, k3.
Work 3 rows st st.
Cont in st st and inc as before on next and every foll 4th row until there are 40(44:48:52) sts.
Cont straight until sleeve measures 14(16:18:20)cm/5½(6¼:7:8)in from cast on edge, ending with a p row.

Shape raglan

Cast off 3 sts at beg of next 2 rows.
1st row K2, skpo, k to last 4 sts, k2tog, k2.
2nd row P to end.
Rep the last 2 rows until 14(16:18:20) sts rem, ending with a p row. Beg with a k row, work 2 rows st st. Cast off.

To make up

Join raglan seams. Join side and sleeve seams.

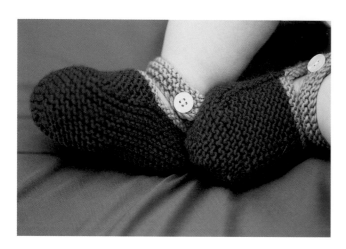

two-colour shoes

These ankle-strap baby shoes, worked in toning shades, can be teamed with the kimono and trousers on page 30.

Measurements
To fit ages
3-6   6-9   9-12   months

Materials
One 50g ball of Debbie Bliss wool/cotton in Main shade (M) and small amount Contrast shade (C).
Pair of 3mm(US 2) knitting needles.
2 buttons.

Tension
26 sts and 56 rows to 10cm/4in square over garter st (k every row) using 3mm(US 2) needles.

Abbreviations See page 7.

Right Shoe
With 3mm(US 2) needles and C, cast on 35(39:45) sts.
K 1 row.
Change to M. Slip first 13(14:16) sts onto a holder, join on yarn to rem sts, k9(11:13) sts, leave rem 13(14:16) sts on a holder.
K 15(17:19) rows for instep. Break off yarn.
With right side facing, k across first 13(14:16) sts on holder, pick up and k12(13:14) sts along row ends of instep, k across 9(11:13) sts of instep, pick up and k12(13:14) sts along row ends of instep, k across 13(14:16) sts on holder. 59(65:73) sts.
K 7(9:13) rows.
Next row [K1, skpo, k24(27:31), k2tog] twice, k1. K 1 row.
Next row [K1, skpo, k22(25:29), k2tog] twice, k1. K 1 row.
Next row [K1, skpo, k20(23:27), k2tog] twice, k1. K 1 row.
Next row [K1, skpo, k18(21:25), k2 tog] twice, k1. K 1 row.
2nd and 3rd sizes only
Next row [K1, skpo, (19:23), k2tog] twice, k1. K 1 row.
3rd size only
Next row [K1, skpo, k(21), k2tog] twice, k1. K 1 row.
All sizes
Cast off.
Join sole and back seam.
With right side facing, 3mm(US 2) needles and C, and beg and ending 6(7:8) sts to each side of back seam, pick up and k13(15:17) sts along heel edge. K 1 row. **
Next row (right side) Cast on 3 sts, k to end, turn and cast on 17(18:19) sts. K 1 row.
Buttonhole row K29(32:35), yf, k2tog, k2.
K 2 rows. Cast off. Sew on button.

Left Shoe
Work as given for Right Shoe to **.
Next row (right side) Cast on 17(18:19) sts, k to end, turn and cast on 3 sts. K 1 row.
Buttonhole row K2, k2tog, yf, k to end.
K 2 rows. Cast off. Sew on button.

classic cardigan

This stocking stitch cardigan knits up quickly in an Aran-weight yarn.
A cotton and silk mixture, the yarn lends the fabric of this classic style
a slight hint of sheen.

Measurements

To fit ages

3-6	6-9	9-12	12-24	24-36	mths

Actual measurements

Chest

52	56	60	65	69	cm
20½	22	23½	25½	27¼	in

Length to shoulder

24	26	28	32	36	cm
9½	10¼	11	12½	14¼	in

Sleeve length

15	17	19	22	24	cm
6	6¾	7½	8¾	9½	in

Materials

6(6:7:8:9) 50g balls of Debbie Bliss
cotton/silk aran.
Pair each of 4mm(US 6) and 4½mm
(US 7) knitting needles.
5(5:5:6:6) buttons

Tension

18 sts and 24 rows to 10cm/4in square
over st st using 4½mm(US 7) needles.

Abbreviations See page 7.

Back and Fronts

Worked in one piece to armholes.
With 4mm(US 6) needles cast on 92(100:108:116:124) sts.
1st row (right side) K3, * p2, k2; rep from * to last 5 sts,
p2, k3.
2nd row P3, * k2, p2; rep from * to last 5 sts, k2, p3.
Rep these 2 rows 1(1:2:2:2) times more.
Change to 4½mm(US 7) needles.
Beg with a k row, work in st st until work measures
12(13:14:17:20)cm/4¾(5:5½:6¾:8)in from cast on edge, ending
with a p row.

Divide for Back and Fronts

Next row K21(23:25:27:29), leave these sts on a holder for
right front, cast off 4 sts, k until there are 42(46:50:54:58) sts
on needle, leave these sts on a holder for back, cast off 4 sts,
k to end.

Left Front

Cont on last set of 21(23:25:27:29) sts only.
Dec one st at armhole edge on 2(3:4:4:5) foll alt rows.
19(20:21:23:24) sts.
Cont straight until work measures 19(21:22:26:29)cm/
7½(8¼:8¾:10¼:11½)in from cast on edge, ending at front edge.

Shape neck

Next row P3(4:4:5:5) sts, place these sts on a holder, p to end.
Dec one st at neck edge on every row until 12(13:14:15:15)
sts rem.
Cont straight until work measures 24(26:28:32:36)cm/
9½(10¼:11:12½:14¼)in from cast on edge, ending at armhole
edge. Cast off.

Back

With wrong side facing, rejoin yarn to next st, p42(46:50:54:58) sts.

Shape armholes

Dec one st at each end of next and 1(2:3:3:4) foll alt rows. 38(40:42:46:48) sts.

Cont straight until back measures same as Front to shoulder, ending with a wrong side row.

Shape shoulders

Cast off 12(13:14:15:15) sts at beg of next 2 rows.

Leave rem 14(14:14:16:18) sts on a holder.

Right Front

With wrong side facing, rejoin yarn to next st, p21(23:25:27:29) sts.

Dec one st at armhole edge on 2(3:4:4:5) foll alt rows. 19(20:21:23:24) sts.

Cont straight until work measures 19(21:22:26:29)cm/ 7½(8¼:8¾:10¼:11½)in from cast on edge, ending at front edge.

Shape neck

Next row (right side) K3(4:4:5:5) sts, place these sts on a holder, k to end.

Dec one st at neck edge on every row until 12(13:14:15:15) sts rem.

Cont straight until right front measures same as Left Front to shoulder, ending at armhole edge.

Cast off.

Sleeves

With 4mm(US 6) needles cast on 30(30:34:34:38) sts.

1st row (right side) K2, * p2, k2; rep from * to end.

2nd row P2, * k2, p2; rep from * to end.

Rep the last 2 rows 1(1:1:2:2) times more.

Change to 4½mm(US 7) needles.

Beg with a k row, work in st st, inc one st at each end of the 3rd and every foll 4th row until there are 44(48:52:56:60) sts.

Cont straight until sleeve measures 15(17:19:22:24)cm/ 6(6¾:7½:8¾:9½)in from cast on edge, ending with a p row.

Shape top

Cast off 3 sts at beg of next 2 rows.

Dec one st at each end of next and 1(2:3:3:4) foll alt rows. 34(36:38:42:44) sts.

Work 1 row. Cast off.

Neckband

Join shoulder seams.

With right side facing and 4mm(US 6) needles, slip 3(4:4:5:5) sts from right front neck holder onto a needle, pick up and k12(13:15:15:16) sts up right front neck, k14(14:14:16:18) sts from back neck holder, pick up and k12(13:15:15:16) sts down left side of front neck, k3(4:4:5:5) sts from left front holder. 44(48:52:56:60) sts.

1st row (wrong side) P3, * k2, p2; rep from * to last 5 sts, k2, p3.

2nd row K3, * p2, k2; rep from * to last 5 sts, p2, k3.

3rd row P3, * k2, p2; rep from * to last 5 sts, k2, p3.

Cast off in rib.

Button Band

With right side facing and 4mm(US 6) needles, pick up and k46(50:54:62:70) sts evenly along left front edge.

1st row (wrong side) P2, * k2, p2; rep from * to end.

2nd row K2, * p2, k2; rep from * to end.

3rd row P2, * k2, p2; rep from * to end. Cast off in rib.

Buttonhole Band

With right side facing and 4mm(US 6) needles, pick up and k46(50:54:66:70) sts evenly along right front edge.

1st row (wrong side) P2, * k2, p2; rep from * to end.

2nd row Rib 2, [yrn, rib 2tog, rib 8(9:10:10:11)] 4(4:4:5:5) times, yrn, rib 2tog, rib 2(2:2:2:1).

3rd row Rib to end. Cast off in rib.

To make up

Sew sleeves into armholes. Join sleeve seams. Sew on buttons.

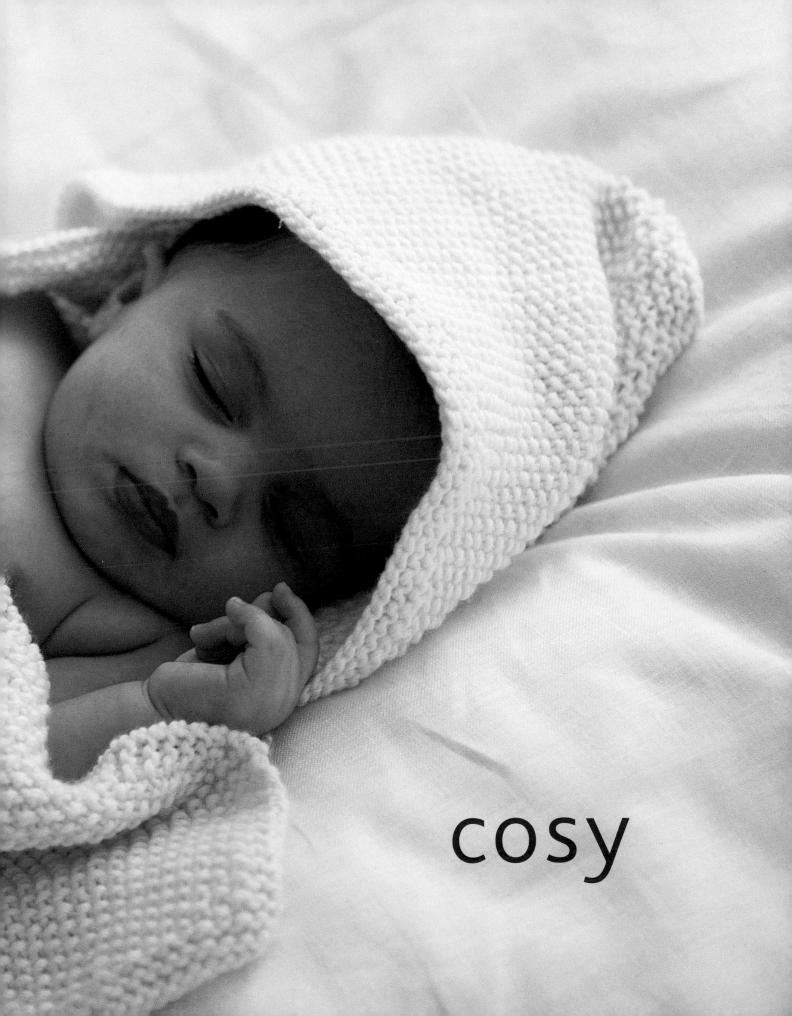

cosy

donkey jacket and shoes

With its warm lining and generous hood with ears, this is a jacket to snuggle into. The shoes are created with double fabric for extra warmth.

Measurements

Jacket:

To fit ages	6	12	12-18	mths
Actual measurements				
Chest	56	62	70	cm
	22	24½	27½	in
Length to shoulder				
	26	30	34	cm
	10¼	12	13¼	in

Sleeve length (with cuff turned back)

	16	18	20	cm
	6¼	7	8	in

Shoes: To fit 6-12 months

Materials

Jacket: 5(6:7) 50g balls of Debbie Bliss cashmerino aran in each of Main shade (M) and Contrast shade (C). Pair each of 4½mm(US 7) and 5mm(US 8) long knitting needles. Two stitch holders. 3 buttons.
Shoes: One 50g ball of Debbie Bliss cashmerino aran in each of Main shade (M) and Contrast shade (C). Pair each of 4½mm (US 7) and 5mm(US 8) knitting needles.

Tension

18 sts and 24 rows to 10cm/4in square over st st using 5mm(US 8) needles.
19 sts and 25 rows to 10cm/4in square over st st using 4½mm(US 7) needles.

Abbreviations See page 7.

JACKET LINING

Back and Fronts

Worked in one piece to armholes.
With 4½mm(US 7) needles and C, cast on 112 (124:140) sts.
Beg with a k row, work in st st.
Work 18(22:26) rows.
1st buttonhole row K to last 6 sts, cast off 2, k3.
2nd buttonhole row P4, cast on 2 sts, p to end.
Work a further 16(18:20) rows.
1st buttonhole row K to last 6 sts, cast off 2, k3.
2nd buttonhole row P4, cast on 2 sts, p to end.

Divide for Back and Fronts

Next row K29(32:36), leave these sts on a holder for left front, k next 54(60:68), leave these sts on a holder for back, k to end for right front.

Right Front

Work a further 15(17:19) rows.
1st buttonhole row K to last 6 sts, cast off 2, k3.
2nd buttonhole row P4, cast on 2 sts, p to end.
Work a further 10(12:14) rows.

Shape shoulder

Next row Cast off 14(16:18) sts, k to end.
Next row P to end and leave these 15(16:18) sts on a spare needle.

Back

With wrong side facing, rejoin yarn to next st.
Work a further 27(31:35) rows.

Shape shoulders

Cast off 14(16:18) sts at beg of next 2 rows.
Cast off rem 26(28:32) sts.

Left Front

With wrong side facing, rejoin yarn to next st.

Work a further 28(32:36) rows.

Shape shoulder

Next row Cast off 14(16:18) sts, p to end and leave these 15(16:18) sts on needle.

Do not break off yarn.

Hood

Join shoulder seams.

Next row With 4½mm(US 7) needles and C, k across 15(16:18) sts of left front, cast on 38(42:48) sts, k across 15(16:18) sts of right front. 68(74:84) sts.

Beg with a p row, work a further 51(53:55) rows.

Shape top

Next row K34(37:42) sts, turn and work on these sts for first side.

Cast off 8(9:10) sts at beg of next and two foll alt rows.

Cast off rem 10(10:12) sts.

With right side facing, rejoin yarn to rem sts.

Cast off 8(9:10) sts at beg of next and two foll alt rows.

Cast off rem 10(10:12) sts.

Sleeves

With 5mm(US 8) needles and C, cast on 28(32:36) sts.

Beg with a k row, work in st st.

Work 10 rows.

Change to 4½mm(US 7) needles. Work 10 rows.

Cont in st st, inc one st at each end of the next and every foll 4th row until there are 42(48:54) sts.

Work 5 rows.

Cast off.

JACKET MAIN PART

Back and Fronts

Worked in one piece to armholes.

With 5mm(US 8) needles and M, cast on 112(124:140) sts.

Beg with a k row, cont in st st.

Work 16(18:20) rows.

Pocket openings

Next row K9(10:11), cast off 15(17:19) sts, k next 63(69:79) sts, cast off 15(17:19) sts, k to end.

Next row K9(10:11), cast on 15(17:19) sts, k64(70:80) sts, cast on 15(17:19) sts, k9(10:11).

Work 0(2:4) rows.

1st buttonhole row K4, cast off 2 sts, k to end.

2nd buttonhole row P to last 4 sts, cast on 2 sts, p4.

Work a further 16(18:20) rows.

1st buttonhole row K4, cast off 2 sts, k to end.

2nd buttonhole row P to last 4 sts, cast on 2 sts, p4.

Divide for Back and Fronts

Next row K29(32:36), leave these sts on a holder for right front, k next 54(60:68), leave these sts on a holder for back, k to end for left front.

Left Front

Work a further 27(31:35) rows.

Shape shoulder

Next row Cast off 14(16:18) sts, k to end.

P 1 row.

Leave rem 15(16:18) sts on a spare needle.

Back

With wrong side facing, rejoin yarn to next st.

Work a further 27(31:35) rows.

Shape shoulders

Cast off 14(16:18) sts at beg of next 2 rows.

Cast off rem 26(28:32) sts.

Right Front

With wrong side facing, rejoin yarn to next st.

Work a further 15(17:19) rows.

1st buttonhole row K4, cast off 2 sts, k to end.

2nd buttonhole row P to last 4 sts, cast on 2 sts, p4.

Work a further 11(13:15) rows.

Shape shoulder

Next row Cast off 14(16:18) sts, p to end and leave these 15(16:18) sts on needle.

Do not break off yarn.

Hood

Join shoulder seams.

Next row With 5mm(US 8) needles and M, k across 15(16:18) sts of right front, cast on 38(42:48) sts, k across 15(16:18) sts of left front. 68(74:84) sts.

Beg with a p row, work a further 51(53:55) rows.

Shape top

Next row K34(37:42) sts, turn and work on these sts for first side.

Cast off 8(9:10) sts at beg of next and two foll alt rows.

Cast off rem 10(10:12) sts.

Rejoin yarn to rem sts.

Cast off 8(9:10) sts at beg of next and two foll alt rows.

Cast off rem 10(10:12) sts.

Sleeves

With 4½mm(US 7) needles and M, cast on 28(32:36) sts.

Beg with a k row, work in st st.

Work 20 rows.

Change to 5mm(US 8) needles.

Cont in st st, inc one st at each end of the next and every foll 4th row until there are 42(48:54) sts.

Work 5 rows. Cast off.

Ears (make 2)

With 5mm(US 8) needles and M, cast on 6 sts.

Beg with a k row, work 2 rows st st.

Next row K3, m1, k3.

Work 1 row.

Next row K3, m1, k1, m1, k3.

Work 1 row.

Next row K4, m1, k1, m1, k4.

Work 1 row.

Next row K5, m1, k1, m1, k5.

Work 1 row.

Next row K6, m1, k1, m1, k6.

Work 1 row.

Next row K7, m1, k1, m1, k7. 17 sts.

Work 7 rows.

Next row K1, skpo, k11, k2tog, k1.

Work 3 rows.

Next row K1, skpo, k9, k2tog, k1.

Work 3 rows.

Next row K1, skpo, k7, k2tog, k1.

Work 3 rows.

Next row K1, skpo, k5, k2tog, k1.

Work 3 rows.

Next row K1, skpo, k3, k2tog, k1.

Work 3 rows.

Next row K1, skpo, k1, k2tog, k1.

Work 3 rows.

Next row K1, sl 1, k2tog, psso, k1.

Cast off rem 3 sts.

Ear Linings (make 2)

With 4½mm(US 7) needles and C, work as given for Ears.

To make up

Join top seam of hood, then join cast on edge of hood to sts cast off at back neck, easing to fit. Join sleeve seams. Sew sleeves into armholes. Using mattress st and matching row for row and stitch for stitch, with wrong side of lining to wrong side of coat, join lining to coat, around all edges. Join lining and coat buttonhole edges together. Sew on buttons. Sew ear linings to ears in pairs and sew to top of hood. Sew cast on edge of pocket opening to lining.

Make a pocket below opening, by sewing main part and lining together.

SHOES

Main Part (make 2)

With 5mm(US 8) needles and M, cast on 3 sts.

Next row P to end.

Next row K1, m1, k1, m1, k1.

Next row P to end.

Next row K1, m1, k3, m1, k1.

Next row P to end.

Next row K1, m1, k5, m1, k1.

Cont in this way to inc 2 sts on every alt row until there are 25 sts.

Next row P to end.

Next row K1, skpo, k to last 3 sts, k2tog, k1.

Rep the last 2 rows until 5 sts rem.

Next row P to end.

Next row K1, sl 1, k2tog, psso, k1.

Next row P to end. Cast off.

Linings (make 2)

With 4½mm(US 7) needles and C, work as given for Main Part.

Heel (make 2)

With 5mm(US 8) needles and M, cast on 3 sts.

Next row P to end.

Next row K1, m1, k1, m1, k1.

Next row P to end.

Next row K1, m1, k3, m1, k1.

Next row P to end.

Next row K1, m1, k5, m1, k1.

Cont in this way to inc 2 sts on every alt row until there are 25 sts.

Next row P to end.

Change to 4½mm(US 7) needles and C.

Next row K1, skpo, k to last 3 sts, k2tog, k1.

Rep the last 2 rows until 5 sts rem.

Next row P to end.

Next row K1, sl 1, k2tog, psso, k1.

Next row P to end. Cast off.

To make up

With wrong sides together, join one lining piece to each main piece. Fold three corners into centre to form an open envelope and sew in place. Fold heel section in half across centre and sew outside edges together, place joined edges of triangle to edges of open envelope, matching points. Sew in place.

hooded blanket

Worked in cashmerino aran, this moss stitch hooded blanket is ideal for wrapping up baby after the bath, or when a summer's day turns chillier.

Measurements
Approximately 66 x 66cm/26 x 26in.

Materials
Nine 50g balls of Debbie Bliss cashmerino aran.
Pair each of 4½mm(US 7) and 5mm(US 8) knitting needles.

Tension
20 sts and 36 rows to 10cm/4in square over moss st using 5mm (US 8) needles.

Abbreviations See page 7.

Blanket
With 4½mm(US 7) needles cast on 133 sts.
K 5 rows.
Change to 5mm(US 8) needles.
Next row K3, * p1, k1; rep from * to last 4 sts, p1, k3.
Repeat this row until blanket measures 65cm/25½in from cast on edge.
Change to 4½mm(US 7) needles. K 4 rows. Cast off.

Hood
With 5mm(US 8) needles cast on 2 sts.
1st row K2.
2nd row K1, m1, k1.
3rd row K to end.
4th row K1, m1, k1, m1, k1.
5th row K to end.
6th row K2, m1, k1, m1, k2.
7th row K to end.
8th row K3, m1, k1, m1, k3.
9th row K3, p1, k1, p1, k3.
10th row K3, m1, p1, k1, p1, m1, k3.
11th row K4, p1, k1, p1, k4.
12th row K3, m1, [k1, p1] twice, k1, m1, k3.
13th row K3, [p1, k1] 3 times, p1, k3.
Cont in this way, inc one st inside the 3 st border, at each end of every alt row until there are 75 sts.
Change to 4½mm(US 7) needles. K 4 rows. Cast off.

To make up
Sew hood to corner of blanket.

cable and rib sweater with hood

This textured sweater has a shawl collar that turns into a hood. It is knitted in a crisp, double knitting cotton to make it the ideal all-seasons top.

Measurements
To fit ages

1	2	3	4	years

Actual measurements
Chest

63	71	81	90	cm
24¾	28	32	35½	in

Length to shoulder

32	37	42	45	cm
12½	14½	16½	17¾	in

Sleeve length (with cuff turned back)

20	22	24	28	cm
7¾	8¾	9½	11	in

Materials
10(11:12:13) 50g balls of Debbie Bliss cotton double knitting.
Pair each of 3¾mm(US 5) and 4mm (US 6) knitting needles.
Cable needle.

Tension
20 sts and 28 rows to 10cm/4in square over st st using 4mm(US 6) needles.
24 sts and 32 rows to 10cm/4in square over patt using 4mm(US 6) needles.

Abbreviations
C4B = cable 4 back, slip next 2 sts onto cable needle and leave at back of work, k2, then k2 from cable needle. See also page 7.

Back
With 3¾mm(US 5) needles cast on 78(88:98:108) sts.

1st and 3rd sizes only
1st row P2, * k4, p2, k2, p2; rep from * to last 6 sts, k4, p2.
2nd row K2, * p4, k2, p2, k2; rep from * to last 6 sts, p4, k2.
3rd row P2, * C4B, p2, k2, p2; rep from * to last 6 sts, C4B, p2.
4th row K2, * p4, k2, p2, k2; rep from * to last 6 sts, p4, k2.
These 4 rows form the patt.

2nd and 4th sizes only
1st row P3, * k2, p2, k4, p2; rep from * to last 5 sts, k2, p3.
2nd row K3, * p2, k2, p4, k2; rep from * to last 5 sts, p2, k3.
3rd row P3, * k2, p2, C4B, p2; rep from * to last 5 sts, k2, p3.
4th row K3, * p2, k2, p4, k2; rep from * to last 5 sts, p2, k3.
These 4 rows form the patt.

All sizes
Work a further 8 rows.
Change to 4mm(US 6) needles.
Cont in patt until back measures 32(37:42:45)cm/12½(14½:16½:17¾)in from cast on edge, ending with a wrong side row.

Shape shoulders
Cast off 21(24:28:33) sts at beg of next 2 rows.
Cast off rem 36(40:42:42) sts.

Front
Work as given for Back until front measures 20(23:26:28)cm/7¾(9:10¼:11)in from cast on edge, ending with a wrong side row.

Shape neck
Next row Patt 31(34:38:43) sts, turn and work on these sts

for first side of neck.

Cont straight until front measures the same as Back to shoulder, ending at side edge.

Next row Cast off 21(24:28:33) sts, patt to end.

Leave rem 10 sts on a holder.

With right side facing, cast off centre 16(20:24:22) sts, patt to end.

Complete to match first side.

Sleeves

With 4mm(US 6) needles cast on 42(42:50:50) sts.

1st rib row K2, * p2, k2; rep from * to end.

2nd rib row P2, * k2, p2; rep from * to end.

Rep the last 2 rows for 4(4:5:5)cm/1½(1½:2:2)in.

Change to 3¾mm(US 5) needles.

Work 4(4:5:5)cm/1½(1½:2:2)in in rib, ending with a 1st rib row.

Inc row P2, * k2, m1, p2, m1, k2, p2; rep from * to end. 52(52:62:62) sts.

Change to 4mm(US 6) needles.

1st row K2, * p2, k4, p2, k2; rep from * to end.

2nd row P2, * k2, p4, k2, p2; rep from * to end.

3rd row K2, * p2, C4B, p2, k2; rep from * to end.

4th row P2, * k2, p4, k2, p2; rep from * to end.

These 4 rows form the patt.

Cont in patt, at the same time, inc one st at each end of the next and every foll 4th row until there are 76(80:92:96) sts, taking inc sts into patt.

Cont straight until sleeve measures 24(26:29:33)cm/ 9½(10¼:11½:13)in from cast on edge, ending with a wrong side row.

Cast off.

Hood

Join shoulder seams.

With right side facing and using 4mm(US 6) needles, k across 10 sts on right front neck holder, cast on 52(56:60:64) sts, k across 10 sts on left front neck holder. 72(76:80:84) sts.

Next row P3, * k2, p2; rep from * to last 5 sts, k2, p3.

Next row K3, * p2, k2; rep from * to last 5 sts, p2, k3.

Rep the last 2 rows until hood measures 19(20:21:22)cm/ 7½(7¾:8¼:8¾)in, ending with a wrong side row.

Shape top

Next row Patt 36(38:40:42) sts, turn and work on these sts.

Cast off 6 sts at beg of next and 4 foll alt rows.

Work 1 row.

Cast off rem 6(8:10:12) sts.

With right side facing, rejoin yarn to rem sts, cast off 6, patt to end.

Complete to match first side.

Right Front Border

With right side facing and 3¾mm(US 5) needles, pick up and k74(82:90:98) sts along right front edge and right side of hood.

1st row P2, * k2, p2; rep from * to end.

2nd row K2, * p2, k2; rep from * to end.

Rep the last 2 rows for 7(8:9:10)cm/2¾(3¼:3½:4)in, ending with a 1st row.

Cast off in rib.

Left Front Border

With right side facing and 3¾mm(US 5) needles, pick up and k74(82:90:98) sts along left side of hood and left front edge.

Work 7(8:9:10)cm/2¾(3¼:3½:4)in in rib as given for right front border.

Cast off.

To make up

With right sides together, fold hood in half and join shaped edge and borders, reversing seam on last 5(6:7:8)cm/ 2(2¼:2¾:3¼)in of border. Sew cast on edge of hood to cast off sts of back neck. Lap right front border over left front border and sew to cast off sts at centre front. Sew on sleeves. Join side and sleeve seams.

circular yoked sweater

This enveloping, generous sweater has a colourful, patterned yoke. All the ribbed edges have a contrasting colour stripe to emphasize the shades in the Fair Isle pattern.

Measurements

To fit ages	2-3	3-4	4-5	years
Actual measurements				
Chest	71	80	89	cm
	28	31½	35	in
Length	40	46	51	cm
	15¾	18	20	in
Sleeve length (with cuff turned back)				
	22	25	28	cm
	8¾	10	11	in

Materials

6(6:8) 50g balls of Debbie Bliss merino aran in Main shade (M) Grey and one ball each in Khaki, Aqua, Red, Fuchsia and Cream.
Pair each of 4mm(US 6) and 5mm (US 8) needles.
Long circular 5mm(US 8) and 4mm (US 6) needles.

Tension

18 sts and 24 rows to 10cm/4in square over st st using 5mm(US 8) needles.

Abbreviations

p2sso = pass 2 slipped sts over.
See also page 7.

Note Read charts from right to left on **every** row. When working Fair Isle pattern, strand yarn not in use loosely across wrong side to keep fabric elastic.

Back and Front (both alike)

With 4mm(US 6) needles and Red, cast on 66(74:82) sts.
1st row K2, * p2, k2; rep from * to end.
2nd row P2, * k2, p2; rep from * to end.
Rep the last 2 rows once more.
Change to M.
Work a further 4(4:6) rows in rib.
Change to 5mm(US 8) needles.
Beg with a k row, work in st st until back measures 21(25:28)cm/8¼(9¾:11)in from cast on edge, ending with a p row.

Shape armholes

Cast off 4(5:6) sts at beg of next 2 rows. 58(64:70) sts.

Yoke shaping

Next row K14(17:20) sts, turn and work on these sts.
Next row Work 2tog, p to end.
Next row Work 2tog, k to last 2 sts, work 2tog.
Rep the last 2 rows 3(4:5) times more. 2 sts.
Work 2tog and fasten off.
With right side facing, slip centre 30 sts onto a holder, join on yarn to rem sts, k to end.
Next row P to last 2 sts, work 2tog.
Next row Work 2tog, k to last 2 sts, work 2tog.
Rep the last 2 rows 3(4:5) times more. 2 sts.
Work 2tog and fasten off.

Sleeves

With 4mm(US 6) needles and Aqua, cast on 38(42:46) sts.
1st row K2, * p2, k2; rep from * to end.
2nd row P2, * k2, p2; rep from * to end.
Rep the last 2 rows once more.

Change to M.

Work a further 10(12:14) rows in rib, inc 4 sts evenly across last row. 42(46:50) sts.

Change to 5mm(US 8) needles.

Work in st st, inc one st at each end of the 5th and every foll 4th row until there are 62(70:78) sts.

Cont straight until sleeve measures 25(29:33)cm/ 9¾(11½:13)in from cast on edge, ending with a p row.

Shape sleeve top

Cast off 4(5:6) sts at beg of next 2 rows. 54(60:66) sts.

Next row Work 2tog, k to last 2 sts, work 2tog.

Next row P to end.

Rep the last 2 rows 3(4:5) times more.

Leave rem 46(50:54) sts on a spare needle.

Yoke

Join the 4 short raglan seams.

With right side facing, 5mm(US 8) circular needle and M, k across 46(50:54) sts from top of left sleeve, pick up and k7(8:9) sts down left side of front neck, k across 30 sts from centre front, pick up and k7(8:9) sts up right side of front neck, k across 46(50:54) sts from top of right sleeve, pick up and k7(8:9) sts down right side of back neck, k across 30 sts from centre back, pick up and k7(8:9) sts up left side of back neck. 180(192:204) sts.

Now work in pattern as follows:

1st round Work across 1st row of Chart 1 to end of round.

2nd round Work across 2nd row of Chart 1 to end of round.

3rd round Using Cream, k to end.

4th round Work across 1st row of Chart 2 to end of round.

5th to 16th rounds Work in patt from Chart 2.

17th round Using Cream, k to end.

18th round Using Cream, k2, * k2tog, k4; rep from * to last 4 sts, k2tog, k2. 150(160:170) sts.

19th round Work across 1st row of Chart 3 to end of round.

20th round Work across 2nd row of Chart 3 to end of round.

21st round Using Cream, k to end.

22nd round Using Cream, k to end.

23rd round Work across 1st row of Chart 4 to end of round.

24th and 25th rounds Work in patt from Chart 4.

26th round Using Cream, * k2, sl 2tog, k1, p2sso; rep from * to end. 90(96:102) sts.

Change to M.

26th round K to end, decreasing 2(0:2) sts. 88(96:100) sts.

Change to 4mm(US 6) circular needle.

Next round * K2, p2; rep from * to end.

Rep the last round 13 times more.

Next row Slip first 33(36:37) sts onto needle, join in Khaki, rib 44(48:50), join in Fuchsia, rib 44(48:50), turn.

Work backwards and forwards in rows, twisting yarns at colour change to avoid holes.

Work 3 rows in rib with colours as set.

Cast off in rib.

To make up

Join side and sleeve seams, reversing last 3(4:5)cm/ 1¼(1½:2)in seam of cuff.

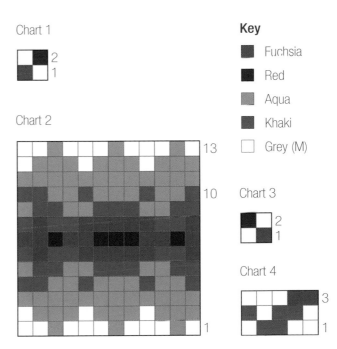

Chart 1

Key

Chart 2

Chart 3

Chart 4

Fuchsia
Red
Aqua
Khaki
Grey (M)

zipped jacket with contrasting edges and hat

With its zipped front opening, pockets and contrasting colour borders, this is a sporty jacket for an active child. For wintry days there is a cosy, ribbed hat.

Measurements

Jacket:

To fit ages	1	2	3	years
Actual measurements				
Chest	69	75	80	cm
	27¼	29½	31½	in
Length to shoulder				
	34	38	42	cm
	13½	15	16½	in
Sleeve length				
	18	22	25	cm
	7	8¾	9¾	in
Hat: To fit	1-2	2-3		years

Materials

Jacket: 6(7:8) 50g balls of Debbie Bliss merino aran in Main shade (M) and one ball in Contrast shade (C). Pair each of 4½mm (US 7) and 5mm(US 8) knitting needles. 35(40:45)cm/14(16:18)in open-ended zip.
Hat: 2(2) 50g balls of Debbie Bliss merino aran in Main shade (M) and one ball in Contrast shade (C). Pair each of 4½mm (No 7) and 5mm(No 8) knitting needles.

Tension

18 sts and 24 rows to 10cm/4in square over st st using 5mm(US 8) needles.

Abbreviations See page 7.

JACKET

Back

With 4½mm(US 7) needles and M, cast on 62(68:72) sts.

K 3 rows.

Change to 5mm(US 8) needles.

Beg with a k row, work in st st until back measures 31(35:39)cm/12¼(13¾:15¼)in from cast on edge, ending with a p row.

Shape back neck

Next row K24(26:28) sts, turn and work on these sts for first side of back neck.

Dec one st at neck edge of the next 4 rows.

Work 3 rows straight.

Shape shoulder

Cast off 10(11:12) sts at beg of next row.

Work 1 row.

Cast off rem 10(11:12) sts.

With right side facing, slip centre 14(16:16) sts onto a holder, join on yarn, k to end.

Dec one st at neck edge of the next 4 rows.

Work 4 rows straight.

Shape shoulder

Cast off 10(11:12) sts at beg of next row.

Work 1 row. Cast off rem 10(11:12) sts.

Pocket Linings (make 2)

With 5mm(US 8) needles and M, cast on 17(19:21) sts.
Beg with a k row, work in st st for 5(6:7)cm/2(2½:2¾)in, ending with a p row. Leave sts on a spare needle.

Left Front

With 4½mm(US 7) needles and M, cast on 32(34:36) sts.

K 3 rows.

Change to 5mm(US 8) needles.

Beg with a k row, work in st st until left front measures 6(7:8)cm/2½(2¾:3)in from cast on edge, ending with a k row.

Shape pocket top

Next row P24(26:28) sts, turn and work on these sts only.

Cast off 4 sts at beg of next row.

Dec one st at shaped edge of every row until 7 sts rem, ending with a wrong side row.

Leave these sts on a holder.

Place pocket

With wrong side facing, rejoin yarn, p rem 8 sts.

Next row K8, then k across sts of pocket lining. 25(27:29) sts.

Beg with a p row, work 13(15:17) rows in st st.

Next row K these sts, then k7 sts from holder. 32(34:36) sts.

Work straight until front measures 29(33:37)cm/11½(13:14½)in from cast on edge, ending with a k row.

Shape neck

Next row P8, slip these 8 sts onto a holder, p to end.

Dec one st at neck edge on every foll alt row until 20(22:24) sts rem.

Work straight until front measures same as Back to shoulder, ending at side edge.

Shape shoulder

Cast off 10(11:12) sts at beg of next row.

Work 1 row.

Cast off rem 10(11:12) sts.

Right Front

With 4½mm(US 7) needles cast on 32(34:36) sts. K3 rows.

Change to 5mm(US 8) needles.

Beg with a k row, work in st st until right front measures 6(7:8)cm/2½(2¾:3)in from cast on edge, ending with a p row.

Shape pocket top

Next row K24(26:28) sts, turn and work on these sts.

Cast off 4 sts at beg of next row.

Dec one st at shaped edge of every row until 7 sts rem, ending with a right side row.

Work 1 row. Leave these sts on a holder.

Place pocket

Next row K across sts of pocket lining, then k8 sts at side edge. 25(27:29) sts.

Beg with a p row, work 14(16:18) rows in st st, ending with a k row.

Next row P these sts, then p8 sts from holder. 32(34:36) sts.

Work straight until front measures 29(33:37)cm/11½(13:14½)in from cast on edge, ending with a p row.

Shape neck

Next row K8, slip these 8 sts onto a holder, k to end.

Dec one st at neck edge on every foll alt row until 20(22:24) sts rem.

Work straight until front measures same as Back to shoulder, ending at side edge.

Shape shoulder

Cast off 10(11:12) sts at beg of next row.

Work 1 row. Cast off rem 10(11:12) sts.

Sleeves

With 4½mm(US 7) needles and C, cast on 30(34:38) sts.

1st rib row K2, * p2, k2; rep from * to end.

2nd rib row P2, * k2, p2; rep from * to end.

Change to M.

Rep the last 2 rows 3(4:4) times more, inc 8 sts evenly across last row. 38(42:46) sts.

Change to 5mm(US 8) needles.

Beg with a k row, work in st st, inc one st at each end of the 3rd and every foll 4th row until there are 50(56:62) sts.

Cont straight until sleeve measures 18(22:25)cm/7(8¾:9¾)in from cast on edge, ending with a p row. Cast off.

Pocket Edgings

With right side facing, 4½mm(US 7) needles and C, pick up and k17(19:21) sts, evenly along pocket opening edge.

K 3 rows. Cast off.

Collar

Join shoulder seams.

With 4½mm(US 7) needles and M, slip 8 sts from holder onto needle, pick up and k15(16:17) sts up right front neck, 6 sts down right back neck, k14(16:18) sts from back neck holder, pick up and k6 sts up left back neck, 15(16:17) sts down left front neck, then k8 from holder. 72(76:80) sts.

Next row P3, * k2, p2; rep from * to last 5 sts, k2, p3.

Next row K3, * p2, k2; rep from * to last 5 sts, p2, k3.

Work a further 5(6:7)cm/2(2½:3)in in rib patt, ending with a right side row.

Change to C.

Work a further 3 rows. Cast off in rib.

Front Edgings

With right side facing, 4½mm(US 7) needles and C, pick up and k66(76:86) sts along right front and collar edge.

K 3 rows. Cast off.

Rep for left front edging.

To make up

With centre of sleeve edge to shoulder seam, sew on sleeves. Join side and sleeve seams. Sew in zip. Sew down pocket linings and tops.

HAT

With 5mm(US 8) needles and C, cast on 86(98) sts.

1st rib row K2, * p2, k2; rep from * to end.

2nd rib row P2, * k2, p2; rep from * to end.

These 2 rows set the rib.

Rep 1st rib row. Change to M.

Cont in rib until work measures 4cm/1½in, ending with a 1st rib row.

Change to 4½mm(US 7) needles.

Work in rib for a further 4cm/1½in.

Change to 5mm(US 8) needles and cont in rib until hat measures 18(20)cm/7(8)in from cast on edge, ending with a 2nd rib row.

Shape top

1st row K2, * p2tog, k2; rep from * to end.

2nd row P2, * k1, p2; rep from * to end.

3rd row K2, * p1, k2; rep from * to end.

4th row P2, * k1, p2; rep from * to end.

5th row K2tog, * p1, k2tog; rep from * to end.

6th row P1, * k1, p1; rep from * to end.

7th row K1, * p3tog, k1; rep from * to last 2(0) sts, p1(0), k1(0).

8th row P1, * p2tog; rep from * to end.

Break yarn, thread end through rem 12(13) sts, pull up and secure.

Join seam, reversing seam on last 4cm/1½in.

cable and moss stitch jacket

Knitted with a soft merino wool, this warm, cosy cabled jacket has moss stitch detailing on the pockets, yoke and collar.

Measurements

To fit ages

6-12	12-18	18-24	months

Actual measurements

Chest

62	70	80	cm
24½	27½	31½	in

Length

30	33	36	cm
11¾	13	14¼	in

Sleeve seam

16	18	23	cm
6¼	7	9	in

Materials

6(6:7) 50g balls of Debbie Bliss merino aran.
Pair of 5mm(US 8) knitting needles.
7 buttons.

Tension

18 sts and 24 rows to 10cm/4in square over st st using 5mm(US 8) needles.

Abbreviations

C4F = cable 4 front, slip next 2 sts onto a cable needle and hold at the front of work, k2, then k2 from cable needle.
See also page 7.

Back

With 5mm(US 8) needles cast on 72(80:88) sts.

1st row (right side) K1, [p1, k1] 3 times, * p1, k4, [p1, k1] 4(5:6) times; rep from * 3 times more, p1, k4, [p1, k1] 4 times.

2nd row [K1, p1] 3 times, * k2, p4, k1, [k1, p1] 3(4:5) times; rep from * 3 times more, k2, p4, k2, [p1, k1] 3 times.

3rd row K1, [p1, k1] 3 times, * p1, C4F, [p1, k1] 4(5:6) times; rep from * 3 times more, p1, k4, [p1, k1] 4 times.

4th row As 2nd row.

5th row As 1st row.

6th row [K1, p1] twice, p3, * k1, p4, k1, p7(9:11); rep from * 3 times more, k1, p4, k1, p3, [p1, k1] twice.

7th row [K1, p1] twice, k3, * p1, C4F, p1, k7(9:11); rep from * 3 times more, p1, C4F, p1, k3, [p1, k1] twice.

8th row As 6th row.

9th row [K1, p1] twice, k3, * p1, k4, p1, k7(9:11); rep from * 3 more times, p1, k4, p1, k3, [p1, k1] twice.

10th to 13th rows Rep 6th to 9th rows once more.

14th row P7, * k1, p4, k1, p7(9:11); rep from * 3 times more, k1, p4, k1, p7.

15th row K7, * p1, C4F, p1, k7(9:11); rep from * 3 times more, p1, C4F, p1, k7.

16th row As 14th row.

17th row K7, * p1, k4, p1, k7(9:11); rep from * 3 times more, p1, k4, p1, k7.

Rep the last 4 rows until back measures 16(17.5:19)cm/6¼(7:7½)in from cast on edge, ending with a wrong side row. Work straight in cable and moss st patt as given for 1st to 4th patt rows, until back measures 30(33:36)cm/11¾(13:14½)in from cast on edge, ending with a wrong

side row.

Shape shoulders

Working 2sts tog over each cable, cast off 21(23:25) sts at beg of next 2 rows.

Cast off rem 30(34:38) sts.

Pocket Linings (make 2)

With 5mm(US 8) needles cast on 16(18:20) sts.

Beg with a k row, work 16(18:20) rows in st st.

Leave sts on a holder.

Left Front

With 5mm(US 8) needles cast on 37(41:45) sts.

1st row (right side) K1, [p1, k1] 3 times, p1, k4, [p1, k1] 4(5:6) times, p1, k4, [p1, k1] 6(7:8) times.

2nd row [K1, p1] 5(6:7) times, k2, p4, k1, [k1, p1] 3(4:5) times, k2, p4, k1, [k1, p1] 3 times, k1.

3rd row * K1, [p1, k1] 3 times, p1, C4F, [p1, k1] 4(5:6) times, p1, C4F, [p1, k1] 6(7:8) times.

4th row As 2nd row.

5th row As 1st row.

6th row [K1, p1] twice, * p7(9:11), k1, p4, k1; rep from * once more, p3, [p1, k1] twice.

7th row [K1, p1] twice, k3, * p1, C4F, p1, k7(9:11); rep from * once more, [p1, k1] twice.

8th row As 6th row.

9th row [K1, p1] twice, k3, * p1, k4, p1, k7(9:11); rep from * once more, [p1, k1] twice.

10th to 13th rows Rep 6th to 9th rows once more.

14th row [K1, p1] twice, * p7(9:11), k1, p4, k1; rep from * once more, p7.

15th row K7, * p1, C4F, p1, k7(9:11), rep from * once more, [p1, k1] twice.

16th row As 14th row.

17th row K7, * p1, k4, p1, k7(9:11); rep from * once more, [p1, k1] twice.

The last 4 rows, form the st st and cable patt with moss st front band.

Patt 7(9:11) rows.

Place pocket

Next row (right side) K7, p1, k4, p1, k2(3:4), sl next 16(18:20)sts onto a holder and work [k5(6:7), p1, k4, p1, k5(6:7)] across 16(18:20) sts of first pocket lining, k2(3:4), [p1, k1] twice.

Cont in patt as set, keeping 4 sts at front edge in moss st, until left front measures 16(17.5:19)cm/6¼(7:7½) in from cast on edge, ending with a wrong side row.

Work straight in cable and moss st patt as given for 1st to 4th patt rows, until left front measures 25(28:30)cm/9¾(11:11¾)in from cast on edge, ending with a right side row.

Shape neck

Next row (wrong side) Cast off 7 sts in moss st, patt to end. Dec one st at neck edge on every foll row until 21(23:25) sts rem.

Work straight until left front measures same as Back to shoulder, ending with a wrong side row.

Cast off rem 21(23:25) sts, working 2 sts tog across cables.

Mark the position for 7 buttons, the first 1cm/½in from cast on edge, the 7th, 1cm/½in below neck shaping with the rem 5 spaced evenly between.

Right Front

Work buttonholes to correspond with button markers on Left Front as follows:

Buttonhole row (right side) K1, p1, yrn, p2tog, patt to end.

With 5mm(US 8) needles, cast on 37(41:45) sts.

1st row (right side) K1, [p1, k1] 5(6:7) times, p1, k4, [p1, k1] 4(5:6) times, p1, k4, [p1, k1] 4 times.

2nd row [K1, p1] 3 times, k2, p4, k2, [p1, k1] 3(4:5) times, k1, p4, k2, [p1, k1] 5(6:7) times.

3rd row K1, [p1, k1] 5(6:7) times, p1, C4F, [p1, k1] 4(5:6) times, p1, C4F, [p1, k1] 4 times.

4th row As 2nd row.

5th row As 1st row.

6th row [K1, p1] twice, p3, *k1, p4, k1, p7(9:11); rep from * once more, [p1, k1] twice.

7th row [K1, p1] twice, * k7(9:11), p1, C4F, p1; rep from * once more, k3, [p1, k1] twice.

8th row As 6th row.

9th row [K1, p1] twice, * k7(9:11), p1, k4, p1; rep from * once more, k3, [p1, k1] twice.

10th to 13th rows Rep 6th to 9th rows once more.

14th row P7, * k1, p4, k1, p7(9:11); rep from * once more, [p1, k1] twice.

15th row [K1, p1] twice, * k7(9:11), p1, C4F, p1; rep from * once more, k7.

16th row As 14th row.

17th row [K1, p1] twice, * k7(9:11), p1, k4, p1; rep from * once more, k7.

The last 4 rows, form the st st and cable patt with moss st front band. Patt 7(9:11) rows.

Place pocket

Next row (right side) [K1, p1] twice, k2(3:4), sl next 16(18:20) sts onto a holder and work [k5(6:7), p1, k4, p1, k5(6:7)] across 16(18:20) sts of second pocket lining, k2(3:4), p1, k4, p1, k7.

Cont in patt as set, keeping 4 sts at front edge in moss st, until right front measures 16(17.5:19)cm/6¼(7:7½) in from cast on edge, ending with a wrong side row.

Work straight in cable and moss st patt as given for 1st to 4th patt rows, until right front measures 25(28:30)cm/ 9¾(11:11¾)in from cast on edge, ending with a wrong side row.

Shape neck

Next row (right side) Cast off 7 sts in moss st, patt to end. Dec one st at neck edge on every foll row until 21(23:25) sts rem.

Work straight until right front measures same as Back to shoulder, ending with a right side row.

Cast off rem 21(23:25) sts, working 2 sts tog across cables.

Sleeves

Using 5mm(US 8) needles cast on 33(37:37) sts.

1st row (right side) [K1, p1] 4(5:5) times, k4, [p1, k1] 4 times, p1, k4, [p1, k1] 4(5:5) times.

2nd row [K1, p1] 3(4:4) times, k2, p4, k2, [p1, k1] 3 times, k1, p4, k2, [p1, k1] 3(4:4) times.

3rd row [K1, p1] 4(5:5) times, C4F, [p1, k1] 4 times, p1, C4F, [p1, k1] 4(5:5) times.

4th row As 2nd row.

These 4 rows form the moss st and cable patt.

Work in patt, inc one st at each end of the 5th and every foll 5th row until there are 49(55:61) sts, taking inc sts into moss st.

Cont straight until sleeve measures 16(18:23)cm/6¼(7:9)in from cast on edge, ending with a right side row.

Working 2 sts tog across cables, cast off in patt.

Pocket tops instructions.

Collar

Join shoulder seams.

With right side facing and 5mm(US 8) needles, starting 3 sts in from front edge, pick up and k19(19:21) sts up right front neck shaping, 29(31:33) sts across centre back and k19(19:21) sts down left front neck to 3 sts from front edge. 67(69:75) sts.

Moss st 1 row.

Next 2 rows Moss st to last 19 sts, turn.

Next 2 rows Moss st to last 14 sts, turn.

Next 2 rows Moss st to last 9 sts, turn.

Next 2 rows Moss st to last 4 sts, turn.

Next row Moss st across all sts.

Moss st 12 rows.

Cast off in moss st.

To make up

With centre of sleeve top to shoulder, sew on sleeves. Join side and sleeve seams. Sew on buttons.

hat with topknot and socks

A neat stocking stitch beanie hat with garter stitch earflaps is teamed with a pair of matching socks.

Measurements

Socks:
To fit   11cm/4¼in foot length
Hat:
To fit ages   3-6   6-12   months

Materials

Socks: One 50g ball of Debbie Bliss merino double knitting in Main shade (M) and small amount in Contrast shade (C).
Set of four 4mm(US 6) double pointed knitting needles.
Hat: One 50g ball of Debbie Bliss merino double knitting in Main shade (M) and small amount in Contrast shade (C).
Pair of 4mm(US 6) knitting needles.
Two 4mm(US 6) double pointed knitting needles.

Tension

22 sts and 30 rows to 10cm/4in square in st st using 4mm(US 6) needles.

Abbreviations See page 7.

SOCKS

To make

With 4mm(US 6) double pointed needles and C, cast on 32 sts.
Arrange sts on needles as follows: first 16 sts on first needle, next 8 sts on second needle and last 8 sts on third needle.
P 4 rounds.
Change to M.
P 10 rounds.
K 1 round.
P 2 rounds.
Next round [P2, k2] to end.

Rep the last round 9 times more.

K 4 rounds.

Shape heel

Working on first set of 16 sts only, beg with a k row, work 12 rows in st st.

Next row K10, skpo, turn.

Next row Sl1, p4, p2tog, turn.

Next row Sl1, k4, skpo, turn.

Next row Sl1, p4, p2tog, turn.

Rep the last 2 rows 3 times more.

Next round On first needle, K6, pick up and k6 sts down heel edge, m1, k2, on second needle, k9, on third needle, k5, m1, pick up and k6 sts up heel edge. 36 sts.

Next round K12, k2tog, k14, skpo, k6.

K 1 round.

Next round K11, k2tog, k14, skpo, k5.

K 1 round.

Next round K10, k2tog, k14, skpo, k4. 30 sts.

K 9 rounds.

Next round K8, k2tog, k1, skpo, k10, k2tog, k1, skpo, k2.

K 1 round.

Next round K7, k2tog, k1, skpo, k8, k2tog, k1, skpo, k1.

K 1 round.

Cont to dec in this way, rearranging sts on needles if necessary and working 2 sts less between groups of decs on every alt round, until 14 sts rem, then dec as set on next 2 rounds. 6 sts.

Break yarn, thread through rem sts, pull up and secure.

HAT

Earflaps (make 2)

With 4mm(US 6) needles and M, cast on 15 sts.

K 1 row.

Next row K7, m1, k1, m1, k7.

K 1 row.

Next row K8, m1, k1, m1, k8.

K 1 row.

Cont in garter st, inc 1 st at each side of centre st on every

foll alt row until there are 27 sts.

Cast off knitwise.

Fold cast on edge in half and join seam.

Hat

With 4mm(US 6) needles and M, cast on 10(12) sts, pick up and k13 sts across row ends of first earflap, cast on 39(43) sts, pick up and k13 sts across row ends of second earflap, cast on 10(12) sts. 85(93) sts.

K 3 rows.

Beg with a k row, work 18(22) rows in st st and dec 0(1) st in centre of last row. 85(92) sts.

Shape top

Next row [K2tog, k5] 12(13) times, k1. 73(79) sts.

Cont in st st, work 3 rows.

Next row [K2tog, k4] 12(13) times, k1. 61(66) sts.

Work 3 rows.

Next row [K2tog, k3] 12(13) times, k1. 49(53) sts.

P 1 row.

Next row [K2tog, k2] 12(13) times, k1. 37(40) sts.

P 1 row.

Next row [K2tog, k1] 12(13) times, k1. 25(27) sts.

P 1 row.

Next row [K2tog] 12(13) times, k1. 13(14) sts.

P 1 row.

Next row [K2tog] 6(7) times, k1(0). 7 sts.

P 1 row.

With two 4mm(US 6) double pointed needles and C, k 1 row. Slide these 7 sts to the opposite end of the same needle, place needle in left hand and bringing yarn firmly from last st to first st, k7 sts.

Repeat this row until a tube of approx 13cm/5in has been worked.

Next row K2tog, k3tog, k2tog, cut yarn, thread end through rem 3 sts, pull up and secure.

To make up

Join back seam. Tie top extension in a knot.

striped sweater

Here's an easy-to-knit, ribbed sweater with a roll collar. As every wrong side row is purled, this is a rib pattern that knits up quickly.

Measurements

To fit ages

1-2	2-3	3-4	years

Actual measurements

Chest

66	76	86	cm
26	30	34	in

Length

32	36	42	cm
12½	14¼	16½	in

Sleeve seam (with cuff turned back)

19	22	25	cm
7½	8¾	9¾	in

Materials

3(4:4) 50g balls of Debbie Bliss merino aran in Main shade Navy (M) and one 50g ball in each of Turquoise (A), Red (B), Fuchsia (C), Lilac (D), Green (E) and Pale Turquoise (F).
Pair each of 4½mm(US 7) and 5mm(US 8) knitting needles.

Tension

19 sts and 24 rows to 10cm/4in square over pattern using 5mm (US 8) needles.

Abbreviations See page 7.

Back

With 4½mm(US 7) needles and A, cast on 63(73:83) sts.
1st row (right side) K3, [p2, k3] to end.
2nd row P to end.
These 2 rows form the patt. Rep 1st row once more.
Change to 5mm(US 8) needles.
Beg with a 2nd patt row, cont in patt working stripe patt as follows: ** 4 rows M, 6 rows B, 4 rows M, 6 rows C, 4 rows M, 6 rows D, 4 rows M, 6 rows E, 4 rows M, 6 rows F, 4 rows M, 6 rows A, until back measures 32(36:42)cm/12½(14¼:16½)in from cast on edge, ending with a wrong side row.
Shape shoulders
Cast off 9(11:13) sts at beg of next 4 rows.
Leave rem 27(29:31) sts on a holder.

Front

Work as given for Back until front measures 27(31:37)cm/10¾(12¼:14½)in, ending with a wrong side row.
Shape neck
Next row Patt 26(30:34), turn and work on these sts for first side of neck.
Dec one st at neck edge on next 8 rows. 18(22:26) sts.
Cont straight until front measures same as Back to shoulder, ending at side edge.
Shape shoulder
Cast off 9(11:13) sts at beg of next row.
Work 1 row. Cast off rem 9(11:13) sts.
With right side facing, slip centre 11(13:15) sts onto a holder, rejoin yarn to rem sts and patt to end.
Complete to match first side.

Sleeves

With 4½mm(US 7) needles and A, cast on 38(43:43) sts.

1st rib row P3, [k2, p3] to end.

2nd rib row K3, [p2, k3] to end.

Rep 1st rib row once more. Change to M.

Work a further 4cm/1½in in rib for cuff, ending with a 1st rib row.

Beg with a 1st rib row, so reversing cuff, work a further 5cm/2in, ending with a 2nd rib row.

Change to 5mm(US 8) needles.

Work in patt and stripe sequence as given for Back from **, inc one st at each end of 2nd and every foll 4th row until there are 52(59:63) sts.

Work straight until sleeve measures 24(27:30)cm/9½(10¾:11¾)in from cast on edge, ending with a wrong side row. Cast off in patt.

Neckband

Join right shoulder.

With right side facing, 4½mm(US 7) needles and M, pick up and k17(16:18) sts down left front neck, patt across 11(13:15) sts at centre front, pick up and k16(14:17) sts up right front neck, then patt across 27(29:31) sts at centre back. 71(72:81) sts.

1st rib row (wrong side) P0(1:2), [k2, p3] to last 1(1:4) sts, k1(1:2), p0(0:2).

2nd rib row K0(0:2), p1(1:2), [k3, p2] to last 0(1:2) sts, k0(1:2). Rib 8 rows.

Next row K0(1:2), [p2, k3] to last 1(1:4) sts, p1(1:2), k0(0:2).

Next row P0(0:2), k1(1:2), [p3, k2] to last 0(1:2) sts, p0(1:2).

Work a further 5 rows as set. Change to A. P 1 row.

Rib a further 3 rows. Cast off in rib.

To make up

Join left shoulder and neckband seam, reversing seam for last 5cm/2in of neckband. Sew on sleeves, placing centre of cast off edge to shoulder seam. Join side and sleeve seams, reversing seam on lower half of cuffs. Turn back cuffs.

bear in lamb sleep suit

Here's a small, tired bear in an all-in-one lamb sleep suit.
The yarn is soft to the touch but hardwearing.

Measurements
Bear approximately 18cm/7in tall.

Materials
Bear: One 50g ball of Debbie Bliss merino double knitting in Camel and small amount in Brown for embroidery.
Pair of 2¾mm(US 2) knitting needles.
Stuffing.
Sleep suit: One 50g ball of Debbie Bliss wool/cotton in Main shade (M) Cream and small amount in Contrast shade (C) Black.
Pair 3¼mm(US 3) knitting needles.
3 small buttons.

Tensions
32 sts and 40 rows to 10cm/4in square over st st using merino double knitting and 2¾mm(US 2) needles.
25 sts and 34 rows to 10cm/4in square over st st using wool/cotton and 3¼mm(US 3) needles.

Abbreviations See page 7.

Note Bear is worked throughout in merino double knitting and 2¾mm (US 2) needles and Sleep Suit is worked throughout in wool/cotton and 3¼mm(US 3) needles.

BEAR

Legs (make 2)
Cast on 26 sts. Beg with a k row, work 5 rows in st st.
Next row P13, turn.
Cont in st st, work on this set of sts only. Dec one st at beg of next row and foll alt row, then at end of foll row. 10 sts.
Break off yarn and rejoin at inside edge to second set of 13 sts, p to end.
Dec one st at end of next row and foll alt row, then at beg of foll row. 10 sts.
K 1 row across both sets of sts. 20 sts.
Work 10 rows.
Next row P10, turn.
Work on this set of sts only. Dec one st at each end of next 2 rows. 6 sts. Work 1 row. Cast off.
Rejoin yarn to rem sts and complete as first side.

Soles (make 2)
Cast on 3 sts. K 1 row.
Work in st st, inc one st at each end of next 2 rows and foll alt row. 9 sts.
Work 6 rows straight.
Dec one st at each end of next row and foll alt row, then on foll row. 3 sts.
P 1 row. Cast off.

Arms (make 2)
* Cast on 4 sts.
Beg with a k row, work in st st, inc one st at each end of 3rd row and foll alt row. 8 sts. P 1 row. * Break off yarn.
Work from * to *.

K 1 row across both sets of sts. 16 sts.

Cont in st st, inc one st at each end of 2nd row and foll 4th row. 20 sts.

Work 9 rows straight.

Next row K10, turn.

Work on this set of sts only. Dec one st at each end of next 2 rows. 6 sts.

Work 1 row. Cast off.

Rejoin yarn to rem sts and complete to match first side.

Body (make 2)

* Cast on 3 sts. K 1 row.

Work in st st, inc one st at each end of next 2 rows and 2 foll alt rows. 11 sts. * Break off yarn.

Work from * to *.

P 1 row across both sets of sts. 22 sts.

Work 12 rows straight.

Dec one st at each end of next row and 2 foll 3rd rows, then on foll alt row. 14 sts.

P 1 row. Cast off.

Back Head

Cast on 3 sts. K 1 row.

Work in st st, inc one st at each end of next 2 rows, then at end of 3 foll rows.

Work 1 row.

Inc one st at beg of next row. 11 sts.

K 1 row.

Break off yarn.

Cast on 3 sts. K 1 row.

Work in st st, inc one st at each end of next 2 rows, then at beg of 3 foll rows.

Work 1 row.

Inc one st at end of next row. 11 sts. K 1 row.

P 1 row across both sets of sts. 22 sts.

Work 6 rows straight.

Next row K11, turn.

Work on this set of sts only. Dec one st at each end of next row.

Work 1 row.

Dec one st at end of next 3 rows. Mark end of last row.

Dec one st at each end of next row. 4 sts.

Work 1 row.

Cast off.

Rejoin yarn at inside edge to rem sts and k to end.

Dec one st at each end of next row.

Work 1 row.

Dec one st at beg of next 3 rows. Mark beg of last row.

Dec one st at each end of next row. 4 sts.

Work 1 row. Cast off.

Right Side Head

Cast on 6 sts. K 1 row.

P 1 row, inc one st at beg.

Work in st st, inc one st at each end of next row, then at beg of 4 foll rows.

Inc one st at end of next row and at beg of foll row. 15 sts.

Work 5 rows straight. Mark end of last row.

Cast off 2 sts at beg of next row.

Dec one st at end of next row and beg of foll row.

* Dec one st at each end of next row and at beg of foll row.*

Rep from * to *. 5 sts.

Work 1 row. Mark beg of last row. Cast off.

Left Side Head

Work as given for Right Side Head, reversing shapings by reading p for k and k for p.

Head Gusset

Cast on 11 sts.

Beg with a k row, work 4 rows in st st.

Dec one st at each end of next row and foll alt row, then on foll row.

Work 2 rows.

Dec one st at each end of next row.

Work 1 row.

K3tog and fasten off.

Ears (make 4)

Cast on 6 sts. Work 3 rows in st st.

Dec one st at each end of next 2 rows. Cast off.

To make up

Join instep, top and back leg seams, leaving an opening. Sew in soles. Stuff and close opening. Join arm seams, leaving an opening. Stuff and close opening. Join centre seam on each body piece. Join body pieces together, leaving cast off edge open. Stuff and gather open edge, pull up and secure. Join sides of head from cast on edge to first marker. Sew in head gusset, placing point at centre front seam and cast on edge in line with second marker on sides of head. Join centre seams of back head, then sew to front head, matching markers and leaving cast on edge open. Stuff and gather open edge, pull up and secure. Sew head to body. Attach yarn about 1cm/½in below top of one arm, thread yarn through body at shoulder position, then attach other arm, pull yarn tightly and thread through body again in same place, then attach yarn to first arm again and fasten off. Attach legs at hip position in same way as arms. Join paired ear pieces together and sew them in place. Embroider face features in Brown.

SLEEP SUIT

Left Leg

With C, cast on 35 sts.

Beg with a k row, work 8 rows in st st.

Shape instep

Next row K26, k2tog, turn.

Next row Sl 1, p3, p2tog, turn.

Next row Sl 1, k3, k2tog, turn.

Next row Sl 1, p3, p2tog, turn.

Next row Sl 1, k3, k2tog, k to end.

Next row P9, p2tog, p to end. 29 sts.

** **Next row** K4, [k twice in next st, k6] 3 times, k twice in next st, k3. 33 sts.

Change to M. Work 11 rows straight.

Shape crotch

Dec one st at each end of next 2 rows. 29 sts. **

Leave these sts on a spare needle.

Right Leg

With C, cast on 35 sts.

Beg with a k row, work 8 rows in st st.

Shape instep

Next row K12, k2tog, turn.

Next row Sl 1, p3, p2tog, turn.

Next row Sl 1, k3, k2tog, turn.

Next row Sl 1, p3, p2tog, turn.

Next row Sl 1, k3, k2tog, k to end.

Next row P23, p2tog, p to end. 29 sts.

Work as Left Leg from ** to **.

Next row K28, k last st tog with first st of Left Leg, k rem sts. 57 sts.

Work 3 rows straight.

Shape front opening

Cast off 3 sts at beg of next 2 rows. 51 sts.

Work 10 rows straight.

Right Front

Next row K12, turn.

Work on this set of sts only for 5 rows.

Shape neck

Cast off 2 sts at beg of next row.

Dec one st at neck edge on next 3 rows.

Work 3 rows straight. Cast off.

Back

Rejoin yarn to rem sts, k27, turn.

Work on this set of sts only for 9 rows.

Shape neck

Next row K8, cast off next 11 sts, k to end.

Work on last set of 8 sts only.

Dec one st at neck edge on next row.

Work 1 row.

Cast off.

Rejoin yarn to rem 8 sts and complete as first side.

Left Front

Rejoin yarn to rem sts and complete as Right Front, reversing neck shaping.

Arms (make 2)

With M, cast on 28 sts. Beg with a k row, work in st st.

Dec one st at each end of 5th row and foll 4th row. 24 sts.

Work 3 rows straight.

Change to C.

Next row K2tog, k3, sl 1, k2tog, psso, k8, sl 1, k2tog, psso, k3, k2tog.

P 1 row.

Next row K3, sl 1, k2tog, psso, k6, sl 1, k2tog, psso, k3.

P 1 row.

Next row K2, sl 1, k2tog, psso, k4, sl 1, k2tog, psso, k2.

Next row P1, p3tog, p2, p3tog, p1. Cast off.

Soles (make 2)

With C, cast on 4 sts.

Beg with a k row, work in st st.

Inc one st at each end of 2nd, 3rd and 5th rows. 10 sts.

Work 7 rows straight.

Dec one st at each end of next row, foll alt row and foll row. 4 sts.

Work 1 row. Cast off.

Neckband and Hood

Join shoulder seams.

With right side facing and M, pick up and k10 sts up right front neck, 3 sts down right back neck, 11 sts at centre back, 3 sts up left back neck and 10 sts down left front neck. 37 sts.

1st rib row K1, [p1, k1] to end.

2nd rib row P1, [k1, p1] to end.

Rib 1 row more.

Next row Rib 4 and slip these 4 sts onto a safety pin, k5, [k twice in next st, k8] twice, k twice in next st, k5, turn, slip the last 4 sts onto safety pin. 32 sts.

Beg with a p row, work 15 rows in st st.

Next row K15, k2tog, k4, k3tog, turn.

Next row Sl 1, p9, p3tog, turn.

* **Next row** Sl 1, k9, k2tog, turn.

Next row Sl 1, p9, p2tog, turn. *

Rep from * to * once.

** **Next row** Sl 1, k9, k3tog, turn.

Next row Sl 1, p9, p3tog, turn. **

Rep from * to * once, then from ** to ** once.

Leave rem 13 sts on a needle.

With right side facing, sl 4 sts from right side of neckband onto needles, pick up and k11 sts along side of hood, k2tog, k9, skpo across sts on needle, pick up and k11 sts down other side of hood, then rib the 4 sts on safety pin. 41 sts.

Rib 2 rows. Cast off in rib.

Buttonhole Band

With right side facing, pick up and k20 sts along right edge of front opening to top of hood edging.

Work 2 rows in p1, k1 rib.

Buttonhole row P1, k1, [yf, k2tog, rib 4] 3 times.

Rib 2 rows. Cast off in rib.

Button Band

Work to match Buttonhole Band omitting buttonholes.

Ears (make 2)

With C, cast on 14 sts.

Beg with a k row, work in st st.

Work 4 rows.

Next row K2tog, k to last 2 sts, skpo. P 1 row.

Dec one st at each end of next and foll 3 alt rows. Cast off.

To make up

Join leg, crotch and centre front seams. Sew in soles. Join arm seams, leaving cast on edge free. Sew in arms. Lap buttonhole band over button band and catch row end edges to base of front opening. Sew on buttons. Fold cast on edge of ears in half and secure, then sew in place to hood.

dressing gown

This is a classic dressing gown. It is knitted in soft cashmerino, for the ultimate in baby luxury.

Measurements

To fit ages

6	12	18	24	mths

Actual measurements

Chest

63	67	72	76	cm
24³/₄	26¹/₂	28¹/₄	30	in

Length

45	51	56	63	cm
17³/₄	20	22	24³/₄	in

Sleeve seam (with cuff turned back)

22	24	26	29	cm
8³/₄	9¹/₂	10¹/₄	11¹/₂	in

Materials

6(7:8:9) 50g balls of Debbie Bliss cashmerino aran in Lilac (M) and one 50g ball in Mauve (C).
Pair each of 4mm(US 6) and 5mm (US 8) knitting needles.

Tension

18 sts and 24 rows to 10cm/4in square over st st using 5mm(US 8) needles.

Abbreviations

kfb = k into front and back of next st.
See also page 7.

Back

With 4mm(US 6) needles and M, cast on 67(73:79:83) sts.
Beg with a k row, work in st st.
Work 6 rows.
P 1 row for hemline.
Change to 5mm(US 8) needles.
Beg with a p row, cont in st st.
Work 37(43:51:57) rows.
Dec row (right side) K3, k2tog, k to last 5 sts, skpo, k3.
Cont in st st, dec one st as set at each end of 4(5:6:6) foll 6th rows. 57(61:65:69) sts.
Work 13(13:13:19) rows.
Shape armholes
Cast off 2 sts at beg of next 2 rows.
Dec one st at each end of next and 3 foll right side rows. 45(49:53:57) sts.
Work 25(27:27:29) rows. Cast off.

Pocket Linings (make 2)

With 5mm(US 8) needles and M, cast on 12(14:16:16) sts.
Beg with a k row, work in st st for 14(16:18:18) rows.
Leave sts on a holder.

Left Front

With 4mm(US 6) needles and M, cast on 34(38:42:44) sts.
Beg with a k row, work in st st.
Work 6 rows.
P 1 row for hemline.
Change to 5mm(US 8) needles.
Next row (wrong side) Cast on 14 sts, p these sts, p to end. 48(52:56:58) sts.

Beg with a k row, work in st st.

Work 36(42:50:56) rows.

Dec row (right side) K3, k2tog, k to end.

Cont in st st and dec in this way at beg of foll 6th row.
46(50:54:56) sts.

P 1 row.

Pocket opening row (right side) K11(12:13:14), slip next
12(14:16:16) sts onto a holder and k12(14:16:16) sts of first
pocket lining, k23(24:25:26).

Work 3 rows.

Dec as before at beg of next row and 2(3:4:4) foll 6th rows.
43(46:49:51) sts.

Work 13(13:13:19) rows.

Shape armhole and collar

Next row (right side) Cast off 2 sts, k to last 2 sts, kfb, k1.

P 1 row.

Next row K3, k2tog, k to last 2 sts, kfb, k1.

Rep the last 2 rows 3 times more. 42(45:48:50) sts.

Work 3 rows.

Next row K to last 2 sts, kfb, k1.

Rep the last 4 rows 1(3:5:6) times more. 44(49:54:57) sts.

Work 17(11:3:1) rows.

Shape shoulder

Next row (right side) Cast off 16(17:18:19) sts, k to end.
28(32:36:38) sts.

Cont on these sts until collar reaches centre back neck.

Leave sts on a holder.

Right Front

With 4mm(US 6) needles and M, cast on 34(38:42:44) sts.

Beg with a k row, work in st st.

Work 6 rows.

Next row (right side) Cast on 14 sts, p these sts, p to end.
48(52:56:58) sts.

Change to 5mm(US 8) needles.

Beg with a p row, work in st st.

Work 37(43:51:57) rows.

Dec row (right side) K to last 5 sts, skpo, k3.

Cont in st st and dec in this way at end of foll 6th row.
46(50:54:56) sts.

P 1 row.

Pocket opening row (right side) K23(24:25:26), slip next
12(14:16:16) sts onto a holder and k12(14:16:16) sts of
second pocket lining, k11(12:13:14).

Work 3 rows.

Dec as before at end of next row and 2(3:4:4) foll 6th rows.
43(46:49:51) sts.

Work 13(13:13:19) rows.

Shape armhole and collar

Next row (right side) Kfb, k to end.

Next row Cast off 2 sts, p to end.

Next row Kfb, k to last 5 sts, skpo, k3.

P 1 row.

Rep the last 2 rows 3 times more. 42(45:48:50) sts.

Work 2 rows.

Next row Kfb, k to end.

P 1 row.

Rep the last 4 rows 1(3:5:6) times more. 44(49:54:57) sts.

Work 17(11:3:1) rows.

Shape shoulder

Next row (wrong side) Cast off 16(17:18:19) sts, p to end. 28(32:36:38) sts.

Cont on these sts until collar reaches centre back neck. Leave sts on a holder.

Sleeves

With 5mm(US 8) needles and M, cast on 29(31:33:35) sts.

Beg with a k row, work in st st.

Work 10(12:14:14) rows.

Change to 4mm(US 6) needles.

P 1 row for hemline.

Beg with a p row, work in st st.

Work 9(11:13:13) rows.

Change to 5mm(US 8) needles.

Work 2 rows.

Inc row (right side) K2, kfb, k to last 4 sts, kfb, k3.

Cont in st st, and inc one st at each end of 8(9:8:9) foll 6th rows. 47(51:51:55) sts.

Work 3(1:13:13) rows.

Shape top

Cast off 2 sts at beg of next 2 rows.

Next row (right side) K3, k2tog, k to last 5 sts, skpo, k3.

P 1 row.

Rep the last 2 rows 3 times more. 35(39:39:43) sts.

Cast off 4 sts at beg of next 4 rows. 19(23:23:27) sts.

Cast off.

Pocket Tops

With right side facing, 5mm(US 8) needles and C, k12(14:16:16) sts from holder.

Cast off purlwise.

Front Edgings

Right front

With 4mm(US 6) needles and C, beg at lower edge, working between 7th and 8th sts from edge and inserting needle through fabric each time, pick up and k one st from each row up right front edge. Note that the same line is kept throughout so at the collar the pick up will be between the 14th(16th:18th:19th) and 15th(17th:19th:20th) sts from edge.

Cast off knitwise.

Left front

Work to match right front but beg at collar edge, working between 14th(16th:18th:19th) and 15th(17th:19th:20th) sts, so ending between 7th and 8th sts at lower edge.

Cast off purlwise.

Cuff Edgings

Fold hem onto wrong side.

With cast on edge facing, 5mm(US 8) needles and C, pick up and k one st from each st along hemline.

Cast off purlwise.

Tie Belt

Cut three 4m/4½yd lengths each of M and C. Knot 3 ends of M to 3 ends of C, smooth yarn out making sure that there are no tangles and knot the other ends together to make a long loop of yarn. With knots lined up in the centre, attach one end to a fixed point and twist the other end until the yarn springs back on itself. Hold the knots firmly and bring the other two ends together, they will twist around each other to make a two colour cord. Knot ends to secure, then leaving 2.5cm/1in tassels, trim cord to 100(105:110:115)cm/ 39½(41½:43¼:45¼)in.

To make up

Matching sts, join shoulders. Graft sts from holders for centre back collar. Sew row ends of undercollar to back neck. Turn facings in to wrong side, join cast on sts at lower edges of fronts, slip st facings in place and sew row ends of collar to back neck. Slip st pocket linings in place. Join side and sleeve seams. Turn up hems. Fold back cuffs.

Make two 6cm/2¼in lengths of crochet chain and sew to side seams at waist level. Thread belt through loops and tie at front.

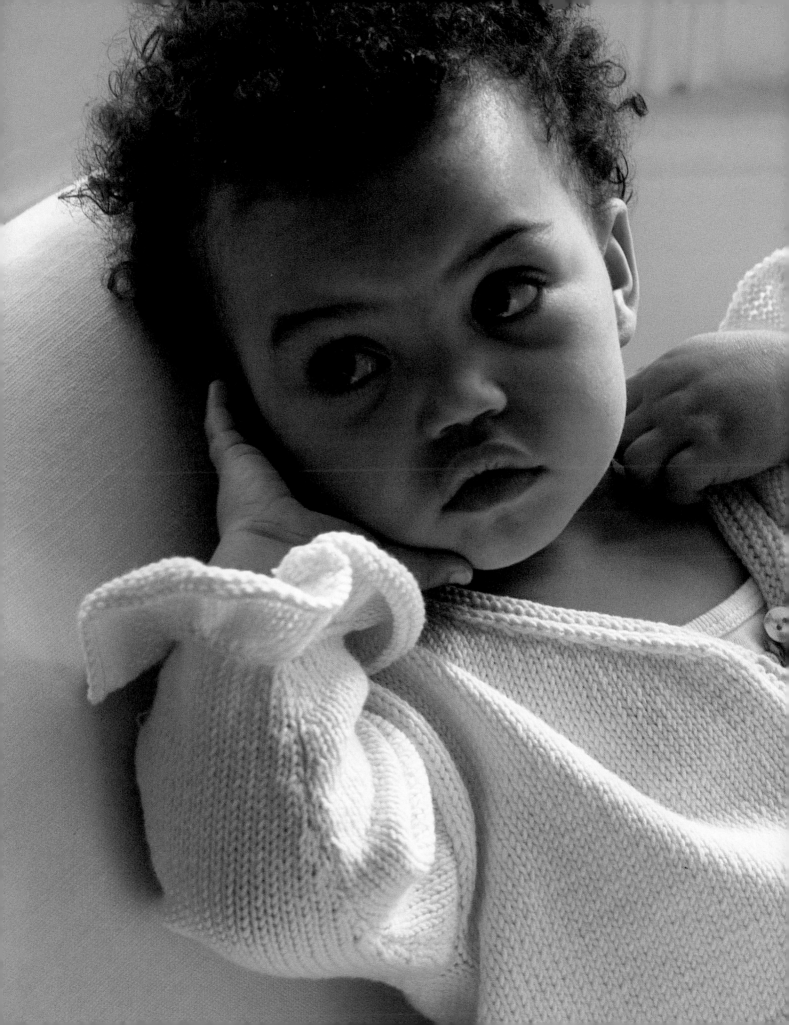

special

beaded fair isle cardigan

A very special cardigan with a delicately shaded Fair Isle yoke enhanced by sewing on toning beads. See page 90 for the matching shoes.

Measurements

To fit ages

3-6	6-9	9-12	months

Actual measurements

Chest

50	56	62	cm
19¾	22	24½	in

Length to shoulder

22	24	26	cm
8¾	9½	10¼	in

Sleeve length

14	16	18	cm
5½	6¼	7	in

Materials

3(4:5) 50g balls of Debbie Bliss wool/cotton in Main shade (M) Pale Pink.
One 50g ball each in Khaki, Dark Aqua, Pale Aqua, White, Fuchsia and Yellow.
Pair each of 2¾mm(US 2) and 3¼mm(US 3) knitting needles.
2¾mm(US 2), 3mm(US 2-3) and 3¼mm(US 3) circular needles.
6 buttons.
74(82:90) small blue glass beads and 37(41:45) small fuchsia glass beads.

Tension

25 sts and 34 rows to 10cm/4in square over st st using 3¼mm(US 3) needles.

Abbreviations See page 7.

Note Read chart from right to left on odd-numbered (k) rows and from left to right on even-numbered (p) rows. When working in patt, strand yarn not in use loosely across wrong side to keep fabric elastic.

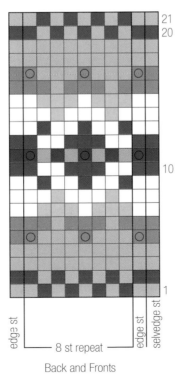

8 st repeat

Back and Fronts

Key

▨	Pale Pink (M)	☐	White
■	Khaki	■	Fuchsia
▨	Dark Aqua	▨	Yellow
☐	Pale Aqua	⊙	Sewn bead

Back and Fronts

Using 2¾mm(US 2) needles and M, cast on 125(141:157) sts.

1st rib row P1, * k1, p1; rep from * to end.

2nd rib row K1, * p1, k1; rep from * to end.

Rep the last 2 rows 2(2:3) times more.

Change to 3¼mm(US 3) needles.

Beg with a k row, cont in st st until work measures 12(13:14)cm/4¾(5:5½)in from cast on edge, ending with a wrong side row.

Divide for Back and Fronts

Next row K31(35:39), leave these sts on a holder for right front, k next 63(71:79) and leave these sts on a holder for back, k to end.

Left Front

Work straight on last set of 31(35:39) sts for 2(4:6) rows, so ending with a p row.

Yoke shaping

Cast off 6 sts at beg of next row, 3 sts at beg of 3 foll alt rows, then 2 sts on 3(4:5) foll alt rows.

Dec one st on every foll alt row until 3(5:7) sts rem.

Cont straight until front measures 22(24:26)cm/8¾(9½:10¼)in from cast on edge, ending at armhole edge.

Shape shoulder

Cast off.

Back

With wrong side facing, rejoin yarn to next st on back holder, p63(71:79).

Work straight on these sts for 2(4:6) rows.

Yoke shaping

Next row (right side) K25(29:33), turn and work on these sts.

Cast off 3 sts at beg of next row, and 2 foll alt rows, then 2 sts on 3(4:5) foll alt rows.

Dec one st on every foll alt row until 3(5:7) sts rem.

Cont straight until front measures 22(24:26)cm/8¾(9½:10¼)in from cast on edge, ending at armhole edge.

Shape shoulder

Cast off.

With right side facing, slip centre 13 sts onto a holder, rejoin yarn to rem 25(29:33) sts, k to end.

P 1 row.

Complete to match first side.

Right Front

With wrong side facing, rejoin yarn to next st on right front holder, p to end.

Work straight on these 31(35:39) sts for 2(4:6) rows.

Yoke shaping

Cast off 6 sts at beg of next row, 3 sts at beg of 3 foll alt rows, then 2 sts on 3(4:5) foll alt rows. Dec one st on every foll alt row until 3(5:7) sts rem.

Cont straight until front measures 22(24:26)cm/8¾(9½:10¼)in from cast on edge, ending at armhole edge.

Shape shoulder

Cast off.

Yoke

Join shoulder seams.

With right side facing, 3¼mm(US 3) circular needle and M, pick up and k41(45:50) sts up right front neck edge, 35(40:44) sts down right back neck edge, k across 13 sts from centre back neck holder, pick up and k35(40:44) sts up left back neck edge and 41(45:50) sts down left front neck edge. 165(183:201) sts.

P 1 row.

Work 1st to 3rd Chart rows.

Dec row (4th Chart row) P5, p2tog, * p7, p2tog; rep from * to last 5 sts, p5. 147(163:179) sts.

Work 5th to 10th rows from Chart.

Change to 3mm(US 2-3) circular needle.

Work 11th to 18th row from Chart.

Dec row (19th Chart row) K3, * k2tog, k2; rep from * to end. 111(123:135) sts.

Work 20th and 21st Chart rows.

Cont in M only. P 1 row.

Dec row K2, * k2tog, k1; rep from * to last 4 sts, k2tog, k2. 75(83:91) sts.

Change to 2¾mm(US 2) circular needle.

1st rib row K1, * p1, k1; rep from * to end.

2nd rib row P1, * k1, p1; rep from * to end.
Rep the last 2 rows once more. Cast off.

Sleeves

With 2¾mm(US 2) needles and M, cast on 36(40:44) sts.
Work 6(8:10) rows in k1, p1 rib.
Change to 3¼mm(US 3) needles.
Beg with a k row, work in st st, inc one st at each end of the
3rd and every foll 4th row until there are 52(58:64) sts.
Cont straight until sleeve measures 14(16:18)cm/5½(6¼:7)in
from cast on edge, ending with a p row. Cast off.

Button band

With right side facing, 2¾mm(US 2) needles and M, pick up
and k55(61:67) sts along left front edge.

Work 4 rows in rib as given for Back and Fronts.
Cast off in rib.

Buttonhole band

With right side facing, 2¾mm(US 2) needles and M, pick up
and k55(61:67) sts along right front edge.
Work 1 row in rib as given for Back and Fronts.
Buttonhole row Rib 2, [rib 2tog, yf, rib 8(9:10) sts] 5 times,
rib 2tog, yf, rib 1(2:3).
Rib 2 rows.
Cast off in rib.

To make up

Join sleeve seams. Sew sleeves into armholes. Sew on
buttons. Sew beads to yoke where indicated on chart.

beaded fair isle shoes

Designed to match the beaded Fair Isle cardigan on page 86, these shoes would also make a perfect gift for a special baby.

Measurements
To fit ages   3-6   6-9   mths

Materials
One 50g ball of Debbie Bliss wool/cotton in Main shade (M) Pale Pink and small amounts of Khaki, Cream, Fuchsia and Yellow.
Pair of 2³⁄₄mm(US 2) knitting needles.
34(40) small pink beads.
2 small buttons.

Tension
28 sts and 40 rows to 10cm/4in square over st st using 2³⁄₄mm(US 2) needles.

Abbreviations See page 7.

Note Read chart from right to left on right side rows and from left to right on wrong side rows. When working in patt, strand yarn not in use loosely across wrong side to keep fabric elastic.

Left Shoe

With 2¾mm(US 2) needles and M, cast on 37(43) sts.

K 1 row.

1st row K1, [m1, k17(20), m1, k1] twice.

2nd and every foll alt row K.

3rd row K2, m1, k17(20), m1, k3, m1, k17(20), m1, k2.

5th row K3, m1, k17(20), m1, k5, m1, k17(20), m1, k3.

Cont in this way, inc 4 sts as set on every alt row until there are 61(71) sts.

K 1 row.

Next row (right side) K6(4), m1, [k7, m1] 7(9) times, k6(4). 69(81) sts.

P 1 row.

Beg with a k row, work 5 rows in st st from Chart.

P 1 row.

Next row K 8(7), k2tog, [k15(11), k2tog] 3(5) times, k8(7). 65(75) sts.

Next row P37(42), p2tog, turn.

Next row Sl 1, k9, skpo, turn.

Next row Sl 1, p9, p2tog, turn.

Rep last 2 rows 5(7) times more, then work first of the 2 rows again.

Next row Sl 1, p to end.

P 1 row.

Cast off purlwise, working 2 sts tog at each corner.

Join back and sole seam.

With right side facing, 2¾mm(US 2) needles and M, and beg and ending 10 sts to either side of back seam, pick up and k21 sts along back heel edge.

K 1 row. **

Next row Cast on 20(23), k to end, turn and cast on 4 sts.

K 1 row.

Buttonhole row K2, yf, skpo, k to end.

K 2 rows.

Cast off.

Sew on button.

Sew beads to the centre row of the Fair Isle band, as indicated on chart.

Right Shoe

Work as given for Left Shoe to **.

Next row Cast on 4 sts, k to end, turn and cast on 20(23) sts.

K 1 row.

Buttonhole row K to last 4 sts, k2tog, yf, k2.

K 2 rows.

Cast off.

Sew on button. Sew on beads as Left Shoe.

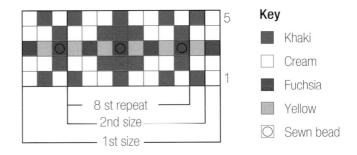

Key

■ Khaki

□ Cream

■ Fuchsia

■ Yellow

⊙ Sewn bead

— 8 st repeat —
— 2nd size —
— 1st size —

dress with lace edging

This vintage style dress has an easy-to-knit lace edging and an eyelet and ribbon tie neckline.

Measurements

To fit ages

6-12	12-18	18-24	24-36	mths

Actual measurements

Chest

52	56	62	67	cm
20½	22	24½	26½	in

Length to shoulder (excluding edging)

35	42	45	50	cm
13¾	16½	17¾	19¾	in

Sleeve length

18	22	24	26	cm
7	8¾	9½	10¼	in

Materials

5(6:7:8) 50g balls of Debbie Bliss wool/cotton.
Pair each of 2¾mm(US 2) and 3¼mm(US 3) knitting needles.
One 2¾mm(US 2) circular knitting needle.
1 button.
61cm/24in narrow ribbon.

Tension

25 sts and 34 rows to 10cm/4in square over st st using 3¼mm(US 3) needles.

Abbreviations See page 7.

Back

With 3¼mm(US 3) needles cast on 97(107:117:127) sts.
Beg with a k row, work in st st.
Work 6 rows.
Dec row (right side) K10(11:12:13), skpo, k to last 12(13:14:15) sts, k2tog, k10(11:12:13).
Work 7(9:9:11) rows.
Rep the last 8(10:10:12) rows until 81(89:97:107) sts rem.
Cont straight until back measures 23(29:31.5:35)cm/ 9(11½:12½:13¾)in from cast on edge, ending with a right side row.
Dec row P4(4:8:2), [p2tog, p4(3:3:3)] 12(16:16:20) times, p2tog, p3(3:7:3). 68(72:80:86) sts.
Change to 2¾mm(US 2) needles.
K 6 rows.
Change to 3¼mm(US 3) needles.
Cont straight until back measures 26(32:34:38)cm/ 10¼(12½:13½:15)in from cast on edge, ending with a p row.

Shape armholes

Cast off 4 sts at beg of next 2 rows.
Dec one st at each end of the next and every foll alt row until 42(48:54:58) sts rem.
P 1 row.

Back opening

Next row K21(24:27:29) sts, turn and work on these sts for first side of back opening.
Next row K2, p to end.
Next row K to end.
Repeat the last 2 rows until back measures 33(40:43:48)cm/13(15¾:17:18½)in from cast on edge, ending with a wrong side row.

Shape neck

Next row K to last 8(8:10:10) sts, leave these sts on a holder, turn.

Next row Cast off 3 sts, p to end.

K 1 row.

Next row Cast off 2(3:2:3) sts, p to end.

Beg with a k row, work 2 rows st st.

Shape shoulder

Cast off rem 8(10:12:13) sts.

With right side facing, rejoin yarn to rem sts, k to end.

Next row P to last 2 sts, k2.

Next row K to end.

Repeat the last 2 rows until back measures 33(40:43:48)cm/13(15¾:17:18½)in from cast on edge, ending with a wrong side row.

Shape neck

Next row K8(8:10:10) sts, leave these sts on a holder, k to end.

P 1 row.

Next row Cast off 3 sts, k to end.

P 1 row.

Next row Cast off 2(3:2:3) sts, k to end.

Beg with a p row, work 2 rows st st.

Shape shoulder

Cast off rem 8(10:12:13) sts.

Front

Work as given for Back until front measures 30(37:39:44)cm/11¾(14½:15¼:17¼)in from cast on edge, ending with a p row.

Shape neck

Next row K16(18:20:22) sts, turn and work on these sts for first side of neck shaping.

Cast off 4 sts at beg of next row.

Dec one st at neck edge on every foll alt row until 8(10:12:13) sts rem.

Cont without further shaping until front measures same as Back to shoulder, ending at side edge.

Shape shoulder

Cast off.

With right side facing, slip centre 10(12:14:14) sts onto a holder, rejoin yarn to rem sts, k to end.

Complete to match first side, reversing shaping.

Sleeves

With 2¾mm(US 2) needles cast on 32(36:40:44) sts.

K 5 rows.

Change to 3¼mm(US 3) needles.

Beg with a k row, work in st st.

Inc one st at each end of the 5th and every foll 6th row until there are 50(56:62:68) sts.

Cont straight until sleeve measures 18(22:24:26)cm/ 6¼(8½:9½:10¼)in from cast on edge, ending with a p row.

Shape top

Cast off 4 sts at beg of next 2 rows.

Dec one st at each end of the next 5 rows, then every 3(4:5:6) foll alt rows. Dec one st at each end of every row until 8(10:12:14) sts rem.

Cast off.

Neckband

Join shoulder seams.

With right side facing and 2¾mm(US 2) circular needle, slip 8(8:10:10) sts from left back holder onto needle, pick up and k9(10:9:10) sts up left back neck to shoulder, 15(16:20:20) sts down left front neck, k across 10(12:14:14) sts from front neck holder, pick up and k15(16:20:20) sts up right front neck to shoulder, 9(10:9:10) sts down right back neck, then k across 8(8:10:10) sts on right back neck holder 74(80:92:94) sts.

Work backwards and forwards in rows.

K 3 rows.

Eyelet row (right side) K3(6:2:3), * k2tog, yf, k3; rep from * to last 6(9:5:6) sts, k2tog, yf, k4(7:3:4).

K 2 rows.

Cast off.

Edging

With 3¼mm(US 3) needles cast on 4 sts.

K 1 row.

1st row (right side) K2, yf, k2.

2nd, 4th and 6th rows K to end.

3rd row K3, yf, k2.

5th row K2, yf, k2tog, yf, k2.

7th row K3, yf, k2tog, yf, k2.

8th row Cast off 4 sts, k to end.

These 8 rows form the patt.

Work in patt until edging, when slightly stretched, fits along lower edge of dress, ending with an 8th patt row.

Cast off.

To make up

Sew on sleeves. Join side and sleeve seams. Make button loop on neckband of left back. Sew on button. Sew edging to hem of dress, joining cast on and cast off edges together. Cut ribbon in half. Stitch one end of each length securely to the inside of back neckband. Thread ribbon through eyelets and tie at centre front.

embroidered jacket

Folkloric-style embroidery is used to embellish this jacket. If you would prefer a simpler look, you could decorate the collar and cuffs only.

Measurements

To fit ages	6-12	12-18	mths
Actual measurements			
Chest	61	70	cm
	24	27½	in
Length to shoulder			
	28	33	cm
	11	13	in
Sleeve length (with cuff turned back)			
	20	23	cm
	8	9	in

Materials

4(5) 50g balls of Debbie Bliss merino double knitting.
Small amounts of wool in Bright Blue, Pale Blue, Cream, Red, Fuchsia, Bright Pink, Dark Green, Mid Green, Lilac and Stone for embroidery.
Pair each of 3¼mm(US 3) and 4mm (US 6) knitting needles.
5(6) buttons.

Tension

22 sts and 30 rows to 10cm/4in square over st st using 4mm(US 6) needles.

Abbreviations See page 7.

Back and Fronts

Worked in one piece to armholes.
With 3¼mm(US 3) needles cast on 143(159) sts.
K 2 rows.
Buttonhole row (right side) K1, k2tog, yf, k to end.
K 2 rows.
Change to 4mm(US 6) needles.
1st row K to end.
2nd row K5, p to last 5 sts, k5.
These 2 rows set the st st with garter st borders.
Work 4(5) more buttonholes from this point to neck shaping, with 5cm/2in between each.
Cont straight until work measures 15(18)cm/6(7)in from cast on edge, ending with a wrong side row.

Divide for Back and Fronts

Next row K37(41), leave these sts on a holder for right front, k next 69(77), leave these sts on a holder for back, k to end.

Left Front

Work straight on last set of 37(41) sts until front measures 23(28)cm/9(11)in from cast on edge, ending at neck edge.

Shape neck

Next row Cast off 3 sts, k next st, p3, place last 5 sts on a safety pin, p to end.
Dec one st at neck edge on every row until 20(22) sts rem.
Cont straight until work measures 28(33)cm/11(13)in from cast on edge, ending at armhole edge.

Shape shoulder

Cast off 10(11) sts at beg of next row.
Work 1 row.
Cast off rem 10(11) sts.

Back

With wrong side facing, rejoin yarn to next st, p69(77) sts.
Cont straight until work measures same as Left Front to
shoulder, ending with a p row.

Shape shoulders

Cast off 10(11) sts at beg of next 4 rows.
Leave rem 29(33) sts on a spare needle.

Right Front

With wrong side facing, rejoin yarn to next st, p to to last 5
sts, k5.
Work to match Left Front, working rem 2 buttonholes and
reversing all shapings

Sleeves

With 4mm(US 6) needles cast on 38(42) sts.
K 5 rows.
Beg with a k row, work in st st until work measures
4cm/1½in from cast on edge, ending with a p row.
K 4 rows.
Change to 3¼mm(US 3) needles.
Beg with a p row, work in st st for 5cm/2in.
Change to 4mm(US 6) needles.
Cont in st st, inc one st at each end of the next and every
foll 3rd row until there are 58(64) sts.
Cont straight until sleeve measures 26(29)cm/10¼(11½)in
from cast on edge, ending with a p row. Cast off.

Collar

Join shoulder seams.
With right side facing and using 4mm(US 6) needles, slip 5
sts from right front safety pin onto a needle, pick up and
k18 sts up right front neck, k29(33) sts across back neck,
pick up and k18 sts down left side of front neck, k5 sts from
safety pin. 75(79) sts.
Next row K to end.
Next row K5, p to last 5 sts, k5.
Rep the last 2 rows 8 times more.
K 4 rows. Cast off.

To make up

Join sleeve seams reversing seam on cuff. Sew in sleeves.
Sew on buttons.

To embroider

Using all the contrast shades, embroider flowers and leaves
in satin stitch, stem stitch, chain stitch and French knots, see
diagrams below and on following page. See page 105 for
stitch instructions.

Key

■	Bright Blue	■	Bright Punk
■	Pale Blue	■	Dark Green
□	Cream	■	Mid Green
■	Red	■	Lilac
■	Fuchsia	■	Stone

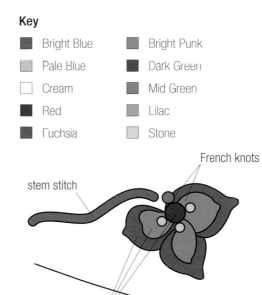

COLLAR EMBROIDERY
(reverse for other collar point)

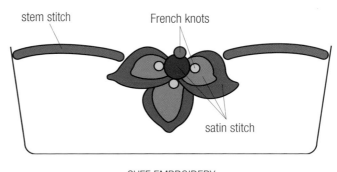

CUFF EMBROIDERY

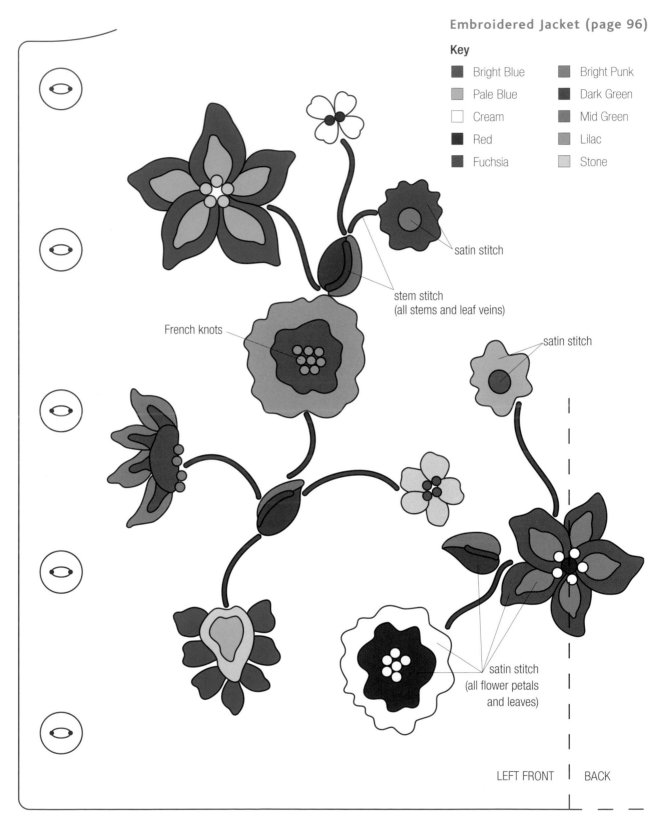

Key

■ Bright Blue   ■ Bright Punk
■ Pale Blue   ■ Dark Green
□ Cream   ■ Mid Green
■ Red   ■ Lilac
■ Fuchsia   ■ Stone

satin stitch

stem stitch
(all stems and leaf veins)

French knots

satin stitch

satin stitch
(all flower petals
and leaves)

LEFT FRONT   BACK

LEFT FRONT EMBROIDERY
(reverse for RIGHT FRONT)

100   special

FRONT NECK EMBROIDERY

Baby's Kaftan
(page 102)

Key

- ■ Fuchsia
- ■ Red
- ■ Turquoise
- ■ Yellow
- ■ Olive

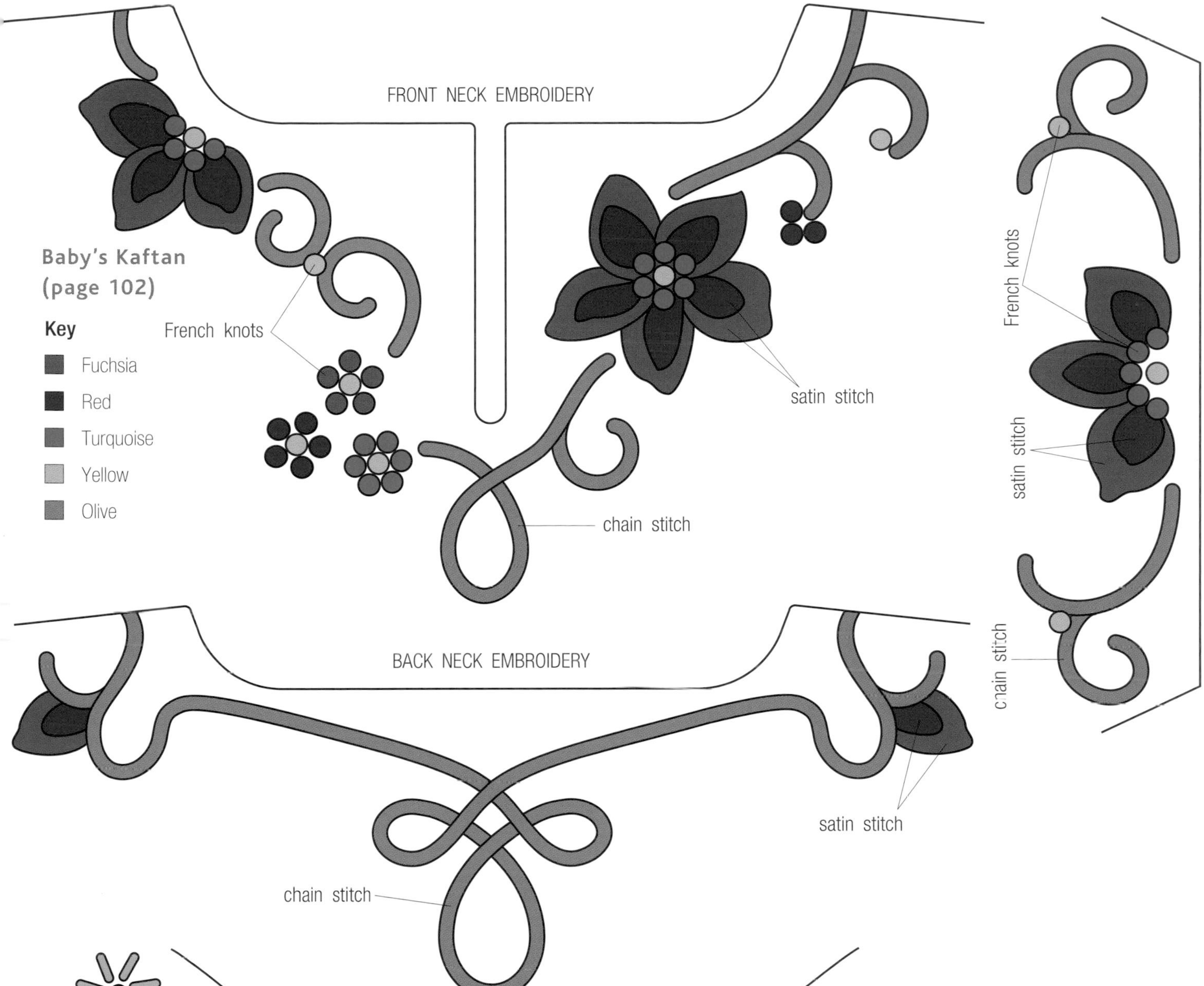

French knots

satin stitch

chain stitch

French knots

satin stitch

chain stitch

BACK NECK EMBROIDERY

satin stitch

chain stitch

chain stitch

chain stitch

TOE OF RIGHT SHOE
(reverse for LEFT SHOE)

chain stitch

chain stitch

satin stitch

satin stitch

stem stitch

stem stitch

satin stitch

chain stitch

satin stitch

French knot

satin stitch

stem stitch

Embroidered Shoes
(page 116)

Key

- ■ Red
- ■ Mauve
- ■ Fuschia
- ■ Khaki
- ■ Yellow
- ■ Duckegg blue
- ■ Turquoise

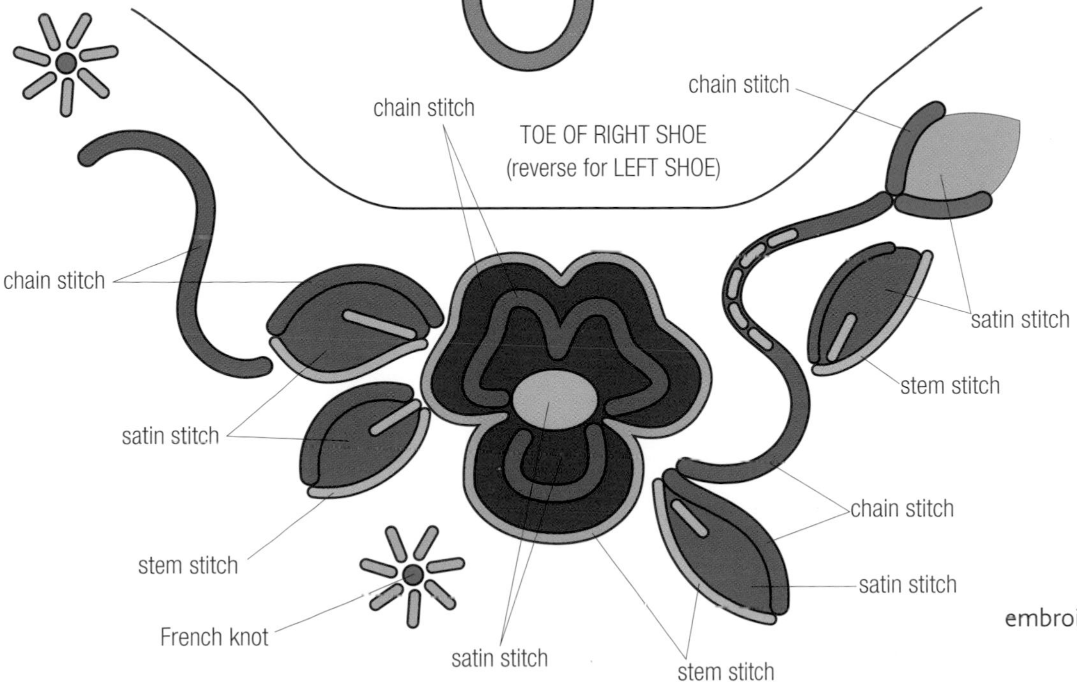

embroidery diagrams **101**

baby's kaftan

Knitted in a cotton mix, this simple V-neck top is decorated with rich floral embroidery to create an Eastern effect.

Measurements

To fit ages

3-6	6-9	9-12	months

Actual measurements

Chest

50	54	58	cm
19¾	21¼	22¾	in

Length to shoulder

11	11¾	12½	in

Sleeve seam

16	17	18	cm
6¼	6¾	7	in

Materials

3(4:4) 50g balls of Debbie Bliss wool/cotton in Main shade (M) and small amounts of wool/cotton in Fuchsia, Red, Turquoise, Yellow and Olive for embroidery.
Pair each of 3mm(US 2-3) and 3¼mm(US 3) knitting needles.

Tension

25 sts and 34 rows to 10cm/4in square over st st using 3¼mm(US 3) needles.

Abbreviations See page 7.

Back

With 3mm(US 2-3) needles cast on 64(68:72) sts.
K 3 rows.
Change to 3¼mm(US 3) needles.
Next row (wrong side) K2, p to last 2 sts, k2.
K 1 row.
Rep the last 2 rows twice more.
Beg with a p row, work in st st until back measures 16(17:18)cm/6¼(6¾:7)in, ending with a p row.

Shape armholes

Cast off 3 sts at beg of next 2 rows.
Dec one st at each end of next and 3(3:4) foll alt rows.
50(54:56) sts.
Work until back measures 26(28:30)cm/10¼(11:11¾)in, ending with a p row.

Shape neck

Next row K16(17:18), turn and leave rem sts on a holder.
Dec one st at neck edge of next 4 rows.
P 1 row.

Shape shoulder

Cast off 6(6:7) sts at beg of next row.
P 1 row.
Cast off rem 6(7:7) sts.
With right side facing, slip centre 18(20:20) sts onto a holder, rejoin yarn to rem 16(17:18) sts, k to end.
Complete to match first side of neck shaping.

Front

Work as given for Back until front measures 19(20:21)cm/7½(7¾:8¼)in from cast on edge, ending with a p row.

Shape front opening

Next row K24(26:27) sts, turn and work on these sts for the first side of front neck.

Cont straight until front measures 25(27:29)cm/ 9¾(10¾:11½)in, ending with a k row.

Shape neck

Cast off 6(7:7) sts at the beg of next row.

Dec one st at neck edge on next 6 rows. 12(13:14) sts.

Cont until front measures same as Back to shoulder, ending at side edge.

Shape shoulder

Cast off 6(6:7) sts at beg of next row.

P 1 row.

Cast off rem 6(7:7) sts.

With right side facing, rejoin yarn, cast off centre 2 sts, k to end.

Complete to match first side of neck shaping.

Sleeves

With 3mm(US 2-3) needles cast on 43(43:47) sts.

K 3 rows.

Change to 3¼mm(US 3) needles.

Beg with a k row, work in st st, inc one st at each end of next and every foll 5th row until there are 59(65:71) sts.

Cont straight until sleeve measures 16(17:18)cm/6¼(6¾:7)in from cast on edge, ending with a p row.

Shape top

Cast off 3 sts at beg of next 2 rows.

Dec one st at each end of next and 3(3:4) foll alt rows.

Cast off rem 45(51:55) sts.

Neckband

Join right shoulder seam.

With right side facing and 3¼mm(US 3) needles, pick up and k15(16:16) sts down left front neck, pick up and k20(22:24) sts down left front opening, k2 centre front sts, pick up and k20(22:24) sts up right front opening, pick up and k15(16:16) sts up right front neck, k5 sts down right

back neck, k across 18(20:20) sts from back neck holder, pick up and k5 sts up left back neck. 100(108:112) sts.

Cast off.

To make up

Join left shoulder and neckband seam. Sew sleeves into armholes. Join side and sleeve seams.

Embroidery

Work embroidery around neck and sleeve edges in colours and stitches as given in diagrams on page 101. See below for stitch instructions.

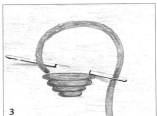
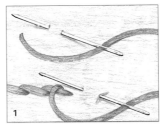
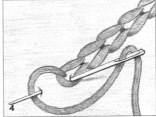
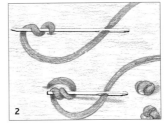

Embroidery stitches

1 Stem stitch Bring the needle and the thread through the knitting, then insert the needle as shown, at a slight angle. Pull the needle through. Continue making short, slightly angled stitches in this way from left the right.

2 French knots Bring the needle and thread through. Wind the thread around the needle twice. Keeping the thread tautly wrapped around the needle, reinsert the needle very near where the thread first emerged and take it through to the back of the knitting.

3 Satin stitch Bring the needle and thread through. Then work parallel stitches close together. The stitches can be made straight across or at an angle depending on the effect desired. Do not pull the thread too tightly or the knitting will become distorted.

4 Chain stitch Bring the needle and thread through. Then reinsert the needle where the thread first emerged and bring it out a short distance away, making sure that it comes out above the thread to form a loop. Continue making loops in the same way.

sheep dress and shoes

This smock-style dress has a trellis-patterned yoke and sheep grazing around the hem. There is a picot edge for a delicate lace effect.

Measurements

Dress: To fit ages

6-9	9-12	12-24	months

Actual measurements

Chest

58	64	70	cm
22¾	25¼	27½	in

Length to shoulder

35	39	43	cm
13¾	15½	17	in

Sleeve length

16	22	24	cm
6¼	8½	9½	in

Shoes: To fit ages

6-9	9-12	months

Materials

Dress: 7(8:10) 50g balls of Debbie Bliss wool/cotton in Main shade (M). One 50g ball each in Black and White.
Pair each of 3 mm(US 2-3) and 3¼mm(US 3) knitting needles.
Cable needle.
Shoes: One 50g ball of Debbie Bliss wool/cotton in Main shade (M) and small amount of Black and White.
Pair each of 2¾mm(US 2) and 3mm(US 2-3) knitting needles.
Cable needle.
2 small buttons.

Tension

25 sts and 34 rows to 10cm/4in square over st st using 3¼mm (US 3) needles.

Abbreviations

C2B = cross 2 back, slip next st onto cable needle and leave at back of work, k1, then k1 from cable needle.
C2F = cross 2 front, slip next st onto cable needle and leave at front of work, k1, then k1 from cable needle.
Cr2L = cross 2 left, slip next st onto cable needle and leave at front of work, p1, then k1 from cable needle.
Cr2R = cross 2 right, slip next st onto cable needle and leave at back of work, k1, then p1 from cable needle.
See also page 7.

Note Read charts from right to left on right side rows and from left to right on wrong side rows. When working colour motifs, use separate lengths of contrast yarn for each coloured area and twist yarns together on wrong side at joins to avoid holes.

Dec row P2(5:7), [p2tog, p2tog, p1] 20(21:22) times, p2tog, p3(5:8). 66(74:82) sts.

Work in patt as follows:

1st row (right side) P4, [C2F, p6] to last 6 sts, C2F, p4.

2nd row K3, [Cr2L, Cr2R, k4] to last 7 sts, Cr2L, Cr2R, k3.

3rd row P2, [Cr2R, p2, Cr2L, p2] to end.

4th row K1, [Cr2L, k4, Cr2R] to last st, k1.

5th row P1, k1, [p6, C2B] to last 8 sts, p6, k1, p1.

6th row K1, [Cr2R, k4, Cr2L] to last st, k1.

7th row P2, [Cr2L, p2, Cr2R, p2] to end.

8th row K3, [Cr2R, Cr2L, k4] to last 7 sts, Cr2R, Cr2L, k3.

These 8 rows form the yoke patt.

Cont in patt until back measures 35(39:43)cm/13¾(15½:17)in from beg, ending with a wrong side row.

Shape neck and shoulders

Next row Patt 23(26:29), cast off next 20(22:24) sts, patt to end.

Work on last set of 23(26:29) sts for first side of back neck.

** Cast off 6(7:8) sts at beg of next row and 3 sts at beg of foll row.

Rep the last 2 rows once more.

Cast off rem 5(6:7) sts. **

With wrong side facing, rejoin yarn to rem sts and patt to end.

Complete as given for first side from ** to **.

DRESS
Back

With 3¼mm(US 3) needles and M, cast on 117(127:137) sts.

Beg with a k row, work 8 rows in st st. Cont in patt.

1st row K5(8:11)M, * work across 1st row of Chart A, k8(9:10)M; rep from * to last 20(23:26) sts, work across 1st row of Chart A, k5(8:11)M.

2nd row P5(8:11)M, * work across 2nd row of Chart A, p8(9:10)M; rep from * to last 20(23:26) sts, work across 2nd row of Chart A, p5(8:11)M.

Cont in patt to end of Chart A.

Work in st st until back measures 22(25:28)cm/ 8½(9¾:11)in from cast on edge, ending with a right side row.

Shape armholes

Cast off 5 sts at beg of next 2 rows. 107(117:127) sts.

Chart A

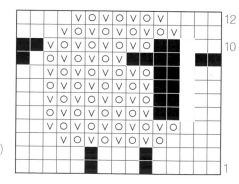

Key

■ Black

□ Main shade (M)

☑ White

◉ White — p on right side rows, k on wrong side rows

Front

Work as given for Back until front measures 30(34:38)cm/
11¾(13½:15)in from cast on edge, ending with a wrong
side row.

Shape neck

Next row Patt 28(31:34), turn and work on these sts for first
side of front neck.

Dec one st at neck edge on every row until 17(20:23) sts rem.
Work straight until front matches Back to shoulder shaping,
ending at armhole edge.

Shape shoulder

Cast off 6(7:8) sts at beg of next and foll alt row.

Work 1 row.

Cast off rem 5(6:7) sts.

With right side facing, rejoin yarn to rem sts, cast off centre
10(12:14) sts, patt to end.

Complete to match first side of neck shaping.

Sleeves

With 3mm(US 2-3) needles and M, cast on 36(39:42) sts.
K 5 rows.

Inc row K3, * m1, k3; rep from * to end. 47(51:55) sts.

Change to 3¼mm(US 3) needles.

Beg with a k row, work in st st, inc one st at each end of the
5th and every foll 4th row until there are 69(77:83) sts.

Cont straight until sleeve measures 18(24:26)cm/7(9½:10)in
from cast on edge, ending with a wrong side row. Cast off.

Collar

With 3¼mm(US 3) needles and M, cast on 96(104:112) sts.
K 3 rows.

Work in patt as follows:

1st row (right side) K3, p4, [C2F, p6] to last 9 sts, C2F, p4, k3.
2nd row K6, [Cr2L, Cr2R, k4] to last 10 sts, Cr2L, Cr2R, k6.
3rd row K3, p2, [Cr2R, p2, Cr2L, p2] to last 3 sts, k3.
4th row K4, [Cr2L, k4, Cr2R] to last 4 sts, k4.
5th row K3, p1, k1, [p6, C2B] to last 11 sts, p6, k1, p1, k3.
6th row K4, [Cr2R, k4, Cr2L] to last 4 sts, k4.

7th row K3, p2, [Cr2L, p2, Cr2R, p2] to last 3 sts, k3.
8th row K6, [Cr2R, Cr2L, k4] to last 10 sts, Cr2R, Cr2L, k6.

Work a further 12 rows in patt.

Cast off 9 sts at beg of next 2 rows.

Cast off 8(9:10) sts at beg of next 6 rows.

Cast off rem 30(32:34) sts.

To make up

Join shoulder seams. Sew sleeves into armholes, sewing row
ends of last 2cm/¾in to sts cast off at underarm. Join side
and sleeve seams. Sew shaped edge of collar to neck edge.

Edging

With right side facing, 3mm(US 2-3) needles and White,
work along cast on edges of back and front, picking up and
casting off at the same time as follows:

Pick up and k2 sts, cast off one st, * slip st used in casting
off back onto left-hand needle, cast on 2 sts, cast off 2 sts,
[pick up and k one st, cast off one st] 4 times, rep from * to
end. Fasten off.

SHOES

Right Shoe

With 3 mm(US 2-3) needles and M, cast on 34(40) sts.
K 1 row.

1st row K1, yf, k15(18), [yf, k1] twice, yf, k15(18), yf, k1.

2nd and 4 foll alt rows K to end, working k1 tbl into yf of previous row.

3rd row K2, yf, k15(18), yf, k2, yf, k3, yf, k15(18), yf, k2.

5th row K3, yf, k15(18), [yf, k4] twice, yf, k15(18), yf, k3.

7th row K4, yf, k15(18), yf, k5, yf, k6, yf, k15(18), yf, k4.

9th row K5, yf, k15(18), [yf, k7] twice, yf, k15(18), yf, k5.

11th row K2, [yf, k4] 7 times, [yf, k3] 0(2) times, [yf, k4] 7 times, yf, k1. 74(82) sts.

12th row (wrong side) Working k1 tbl into yf of previous row, work as follows: k4, [p2, k6] to last 6 sts, p2, k4.

Beg with a 1st patt row, work 9 rows in yoke patt as given for Back of dress.

Next row (wrong side) K4, [p2tog, k6] to last 6 sts, p2tog, k4. 65(72) sts.

Shape instep

1st size only

1st row K38, skpo, turn.

2nd size only

1st row K35, k2tog, k5, turn.

Both sizes

2nd row Sl 1, p11, p2tog, turn.

3rd row Sl 1, k11, skpo, turn.

4th row Sl 1, p11, p2tog, turn.

5th row Sl 1, k acoss 1st row of Chart B, skpo, turn.

6th row Sl 1, p across 2nd row of Chart B, skpo, turn.

7th to 12th rows Rep 5th and 6th rows 3 times, working 3rd to 8th rows of Chart B.

Rep 3rd and 4th rows 2(3) times more.

Next row Sl 1, k to end.

Cast off, decreasing one st at each corner.

Join sole and back seam.

With right side facing, 3mm(US 2-3) needles and beginning and ending 8 sts at either side of back seam, pick up and k17 sts along heel edge. K 1 row. **

Next row Cast on 3 sts, k to end, turn and cast on 19 sts.
K 1 row.

Buttonhole row K35, yf, k2tog, k2.
K 2 rows. Cast off.

Edging

With right side facing, 2¾mm(US 2) needles and White, work around top edge of shoe and pick up and cast off at the same time as follows: Pick up and k2 sts, cast off one st, * slip st used in casting off back onto left-hand needle, cast on 2 sts, cast off 2 sts, [pick up and k one st, cast off one st] 4 times, rep from * to end. Fasten off. Sew on button.

Left Shoe

Work as given for Right Shoe to **, working from Chart C instead of Chart B.

Next row Cast on 19 sts, k to end, turn and cast on 3 sts.
K 1 row.

Buttonhole row K2, k2tog, yf, k to end.
K 2 rows. Cast off.

Edging

With right side facing, 2¾mm(US 2) needles and White, work around top edge of shoe and pick up and cast off at the same time as follows: Pick up and k2 sts, cast off one st, * slip st used in casting off back onto left-hand needle, cast on 2 sts, cast off 2 sts, [pick up and k one st, cast off one st] 4 times, rep from * to end. Fasten off. Sew on button.

Chart B

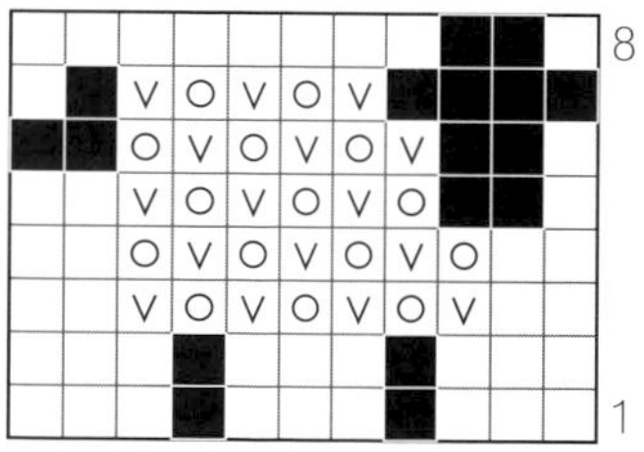

Chart C

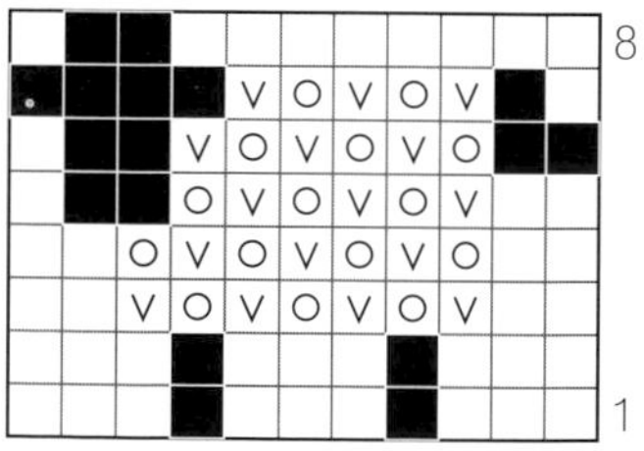

Key

■ Black   V White

☐ Main shade (M)   ⊙ White – p on right side rows, k on wrong side rows

cardigan with frilled sleeves

The flounce on the sleeves of this simple stocking stitch cardigan gives it a party feel. It is knitted in a soft wool and cotton mix.

Measurements

To fit ages

9-12	12-18	24-36	months

Actual measurements

Chest

62	70	76	cm
24½	27½	30	in

Length to shoulder

28	32	36	cm
11	12½	14¼	in

Sleeve length (including frill)

15	17	19	cm
6	6¾	7½	in

Materials

4(4:5) 50g balls of Debbie Bliss wool/cotton.
Pair each of 2¾mm(US 2), 3¼mm (US 3) and 3¾mm(US 5) knitting needles.
Long 3¼mm(US 3) circular knitting needle.
2 stitch holders.
6(6:7) buttons.

Tension

25 sts and 34 rows to 10cm/4in square over st st using 3¼mm(US 3) needles.

Abbreviations See page 7.

Back and Fronts

Worked in one piece to armholes.
With 2¾mm(US 2) needles cast on 156(176:192) sts.
K 4 rows.
Change to 3¼mm(US 3) needles.
Beg with a k row, work in st st until work measures 16(19:22)cm/6¼(7½:8¾)in from cast on edge, ending with a p row.

Divide for Back and Fronts

Next row K39(44:48) sts, leave these sts on a holder for right front, k next 78(88:96) sts, leave these sts on a holder for back, k to end.

Left Front

Work straight on last set of 39(44:48) sts until front measures 20(23:26)cm/8(9:10¼)in from cast on edge, ending with a p row.

Shape neck

Next row K to last 4 sts, k2tog, k2.
Next row P2, p2tog, p to end.
Dec one st at neck edge on every row until 20(24:27) sts rem.
Work straight until front measures 28(32:36)cm/11(12½:14¼)in from cast on edge, ending with a p row.

Shape shoulder

Cast off 10(12:13) sts beg of next row.
P 1 row.
Cast off rem 10(12:14) sts.

Back

With wrong side facing, rejoin yarn to next st on holder, p78(88:96) sts, turn.
Work on this set of sts only until back measures same

as Left Front to shoulder shaping, ending with a p row.

Shape shoulder

Cast off 10(12:13) sts at beg of next 2 rows.

Cast off 10(12:14) sts at beg of foll 2 rows.

Cast off rem 38(40:42) sts.

Right Front

With wrong side facing, rejoin yarn to rem sts on holder, p to end.

Cont in st st until work measures 20(23:26)cm/8(9:10¼)in from cast on edge, ending with a p row.

Shape neck

Next row K2, skpo, k to end.

Next row P to last 4 sts, p2togtbl, p2.

Complete to match left front.

Sleeves

With 2¾mm(US 2) needles, cast on 42(46:52) sts.

K 2 rows.

Change to 3¼mm(US 3) needles.

Beg with a k row, work in st st, inc one st at each end of every foll 4th(5th:5th) row until there are 61(66:72) sts.

Cont straight until sleeve measures 14(16:18)cm/5¼(6¼:7)in from cast on edge, ending with a p row.

Cast off.

Front and Neck Bands

Join shoulder seams.

With right side facing and 3¼mm(US 3) circular needle, pick up and k49(57:65) sts up right front edge to beg of neck shaping, 27(29:33) sts up right front neck to shoulder seam, 28(30:32) sts across back neck edge, 27(29:33) sts down left front neck to beg of neck shaping and 49(57:65) sts down left front to cast on edge. 180(202:228) sts.

Next row K to end.

Next row K1(2:2), k2tog, yf, [k7(8:8), k2tog, yf] 5(5:6) times, k to end.

Next row K to end.

Cast off.

Sleeve Edgings

With right side facing and 3¼mm(US 3) needles, pick up and k42(46:52) sts along lower edge of sleeve.

Next row P1, [inc in next st] 40(44:50) times, p1.

Beg with a k row, work 6 rows in st st.

Change to 3¾mm(US 5) needles.

Work a further 4 rows.

Cast off.

To make up

Join sleeve seams. Sew sleeves into armholes.

Sew on buttons.

fair isle bag

The perfect baby accessory to decorate the nursery, this pretty baby bag has a beaded picot edge.

Measurements
Approximately 17 x 20cm/7 x 8in.

Materials
One 50g ball of Debbie Bliss wool/cotton in each of Main shade Pale Pink (M), Brown, Dark Aqua, Cream and Dark Red, and small amount of Yellow.
Pair of 3¼mm(US 3) knitting needles.
29 small knitting beads.

Tension
25 sts and 34 rows to 10cm/4in square over st st using 3¼mm(US 3) needles.

Abbreviations See page 7.

Note Read chart from right to left on right side rows and from left to right on wrong side rows. When working in patt, strand yarn not in use loosely across wrong side to keep fabric elastic.

To make

Thread the beads onto M and with 3¼mm(US 3) needles, work a beaded picot cast on edge as follows: [Cast on 5 sts, k1, bring yarn and 1 bead forward to the front of the work, slip 1 st purlwise, then holding bead to the front, take yarn back and pass k st over sl st, k1, cast off 1, place rem st on right-hand needle back onto left-hand needle] 29 times, cast on 2 sts. 89 sts.

Beg with a k row, work in st st.

Work 6 rows.

Dec row K9, [k2tog, k21] 3 times, k2tog, k9. 85 sts.

P 1 row.

Eyelet row K3, [k2tog, yf, k5] 11 times, k2tog, yf, k3.

Work 3 rows.

Inc row K9, [m1, k22] 3 times, m1, k10. 89 sts.

Work 3 rows.

Beg with a k row, cont in st st and work 37 rows from Chart, working the edge st at beg of k rows and the end of p rows and repeating the 8 patt sts across the row.

Cont in Brown only.

P 1 row.

Shape base

Next row (right side) K1, [k2tog, k6] to end. 78 sts.

P 1 row.

Next row K1, [k2tog, k5] to end. 67 sts.

P 1 row.

Cont to decrease in this way working one less st between decreases on every alt row until 12 sts rem.

Break yarn, thread through sts, pull up and secure.

Join seam.

Drawstrings (make 2)

With Brown, make two 51cm/20in long narrow plaits. Thread through the eyelets, the first plait starting and ending either side of the seam, the second directly opposite. Tie the plait ends together and pull up to close the bag.

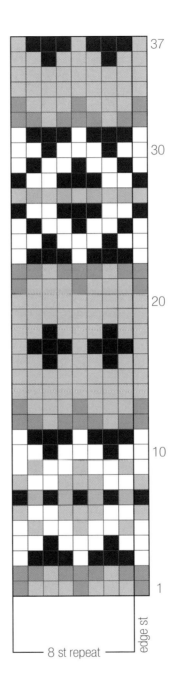

37

30

20

10

1

edge st

8 st repeat

Key

- Pale Pink (M)
- Brown
- Dark Aqua
- Cream
- Dark Red
- Yellow

embroidered shoes

Inspired by Chinese slippers, these knitted shoes are embellished with sumptuous flowers and leaves.

Measurements
To fit age   6-12   months

Materials
One 50g ball of Debbie Bliss wool/cotton in Main shade (M) and small amounts of Red, Mauve, Fuchsia, Khaki, Yellow, Duckegg Blue and Turquoise for embroidery.
Pair of 3¼mm(US 3) knitting needles.

Tension
30 sts and 52 rows to 10cm/4in square over garter st (k every row) using 3¼mm(US 3) needles.

Abbreviations See page 7.

To make
With 3¼mm(US 3) needles and M, cast on 13 sts for top.
K 20 rows. Leave sts on a holder.
With 3¼mm(US 3) needles and M, cast on 17 sts, with right side facing, pick up and k14 sts along right edge of top, k13 sts from holder, pick up and k14 sts along left edge of top, turn and cast on 17 sts. 75 sts.
K 11 rows.

Shape sole

1st row Sl 1, k32, k2tog, k5, k2tog, k to end.

2nd row Sl 1, k31, k2tog, k5, k2tog, k to end.

3rd row Sl 1, k2, k2tog, k24, k2tog, k3, k3tog, k3, k2tog, k24, k2tog, k3.

4th and 5th rows Sl 1, k to end.

6th row K2tog, [k3, k2tog, k22, k2tog] twice, k3, k2tog.

7th and 8th rows Sl 1, k to end.

9th row K2tog, k2, k2tog, k18, [k2tog, k1] 4 times, k17, k2tog, k2, k2tog.

10th row Sl 1, k to end.

11th row Sl 1, [k2tog, k1] 3 times, k10, [k2tog, k1] 4 times, k10, [k2tog, k1] 3 times. 41 sts. Cast off.

To make up
Join back and sole seam.

To embroider
Using all the contrast shades, embroider flowers and leaves in satin stitch, stem stitch, chain stitch, backstitch and French knots on right shoe (see diagram on page 101), then work a mirror image on the left shoe.
See page 105 for stitch instructions.

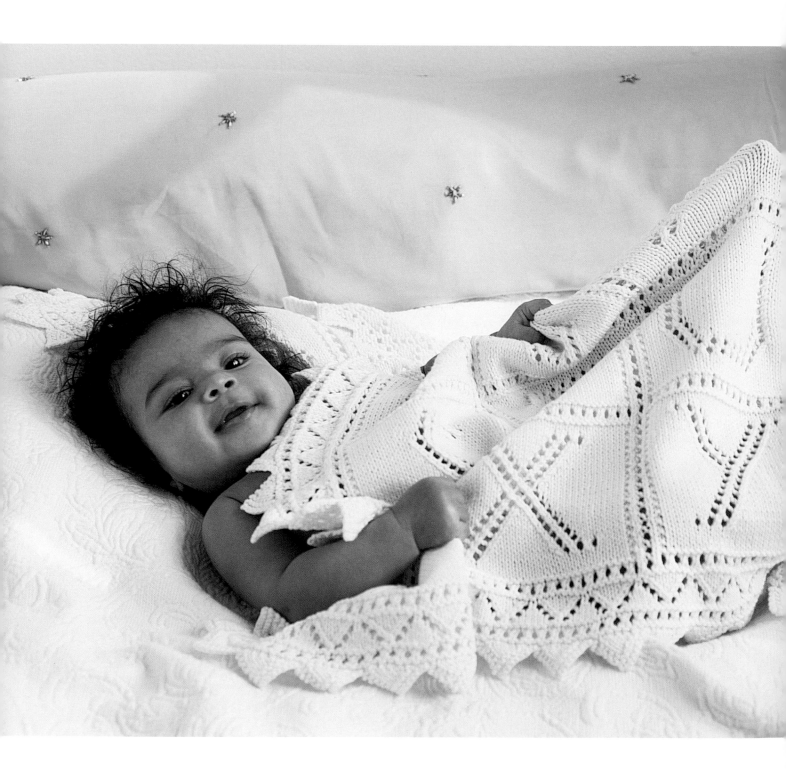

alphabet blanket

The alphabet is picked out in delicate lace stitches in this intricately worked blanket designed for a cherished baby. It is enhanced by a pretty decorative edging.

Measurements
Approximately 90 x 90cm/35½ x 35½in.

Materials
Eleven 50g balls of Debbie Bliss wool/cotton.
Pair each of long 2¾mm(US 2) and 3¼mm(US 3) knitting needles or circular needles.

Tension
25 sts and 34 rows to 10cm/4in square over st st using 3¼mm(US 3) needles.

Abbreviations See page 7.

Chart note Read chart from right to left on right side rows and from left to right on wrong side rows.

Note If working on circular needles, work in rows not rounds.
For a completely flat finish to the edging, use a smooth contrast colour yarn to cast on, and when completed, do not cast off, leave sts on the needle and cont to work top border on these sts. To work the lower border, undo the cast on row, placing the loops on a 3¼mm(US 3) circular or long needle.

To make
Using 3¼mm(US 3) long or circular needle, loosely cast on 187 sts.
Beg with 1st row, work in patt from Alphabet Blocks Chart on pages 120–123. Cast off (see Note).

Top Border
With right side facing and 3¼mm(US 3) long or circular needle, pick up and k187 sts. P 1 row. Omit the last 2 rows if sts have been left on needle.
Work 12 rows of Border Chart. 199 sts.
Transfer sts to 2¾mm(US 2) long or circular needle.

Triangle edging
1st row (right side) P1, turn. **2nd row** P1. **3rd row** P2, turn. **4th row** P2. **5th row** P2, k1, turn. **6th row** P3. **7th row** P2, k2, turn. **8th row** P4. **9th row** P2, k3, turn. **10th row** P5. **11th row** P2, k4, turn. **12th row** P6. **13th row** P7, turn. **14th row** P7. **15th row** Cast off 8 sts purlwise, one st on right needle, turn.
Rep 2nd to 15th rows, until 15th row of last triangle, then cast off rem 7 sts.

Lower Border
With right side facing and 3¼mm(US 3) long or circular needle, pick up and k187 sts. P 1 row.
Omit the last 2 rows if cast on sts have been undone.
Work 12 rows of Border Chart. 199 sts.
Transfer sts to 2¾mm(US 2) long or circular needle and work triangle edging as given for Top Border.

Side Borders
With right side facing and 3¼mm(US 3) long or circular needle, pick up and k227 sts along right side edge. Work 12 rows of Border Chart. 239 sts.
Transfer sts onto a 2¾mm(US 2) long or circular needle and work triangle edging as given for Top Border.
Work border along left side as given for right side.

To make up
Join corner seams.

Key

- ☐ k on right side rows, p on wrong side rows
- • p on right side rows
- ╱ k2tog on right side rows, p2tog on wrong side rows
- ╲ skpo
- ○ yarn over needle to make a stitch
- ◿ k3tog
- ◸ slip 1, k2tog, psso

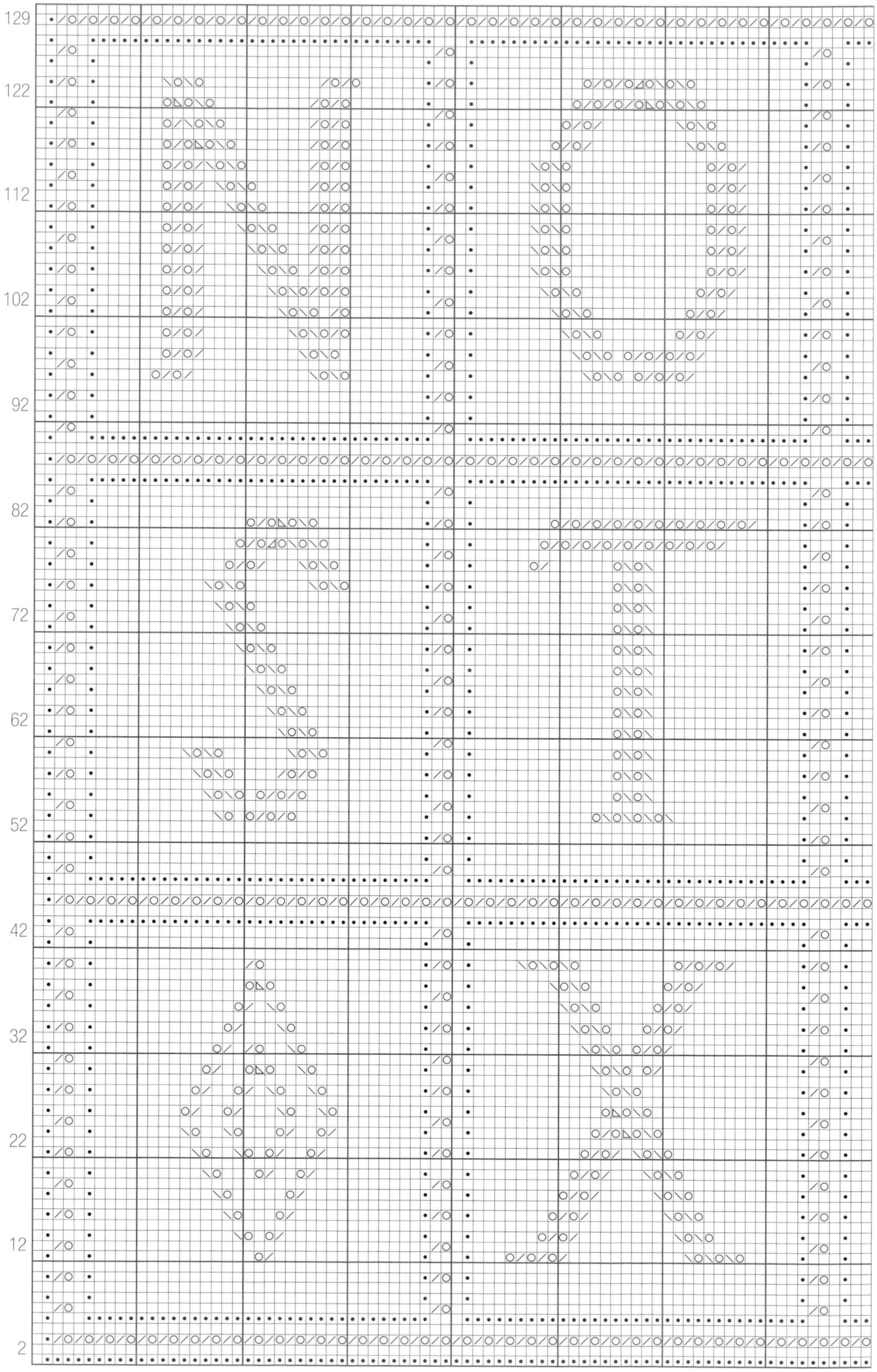

129

122

112

102

92

82

72

62

52

42

32

22

12

2

120   special

Note Read each chart row all the way across this page and the page opposite. Chart continues on next two pages.

Key

☐	k on right side rows, p on wrong side rows
•	p on right side rows
╱	k2tog on right side rows, p2tog on wrong side rows
╲	skpo
○	yarn over needle to make a stitch
◢	k3tog
◣	slip 1, k2tog, psso

Border Chart

edge sts · repeat 8 sts · edge sts

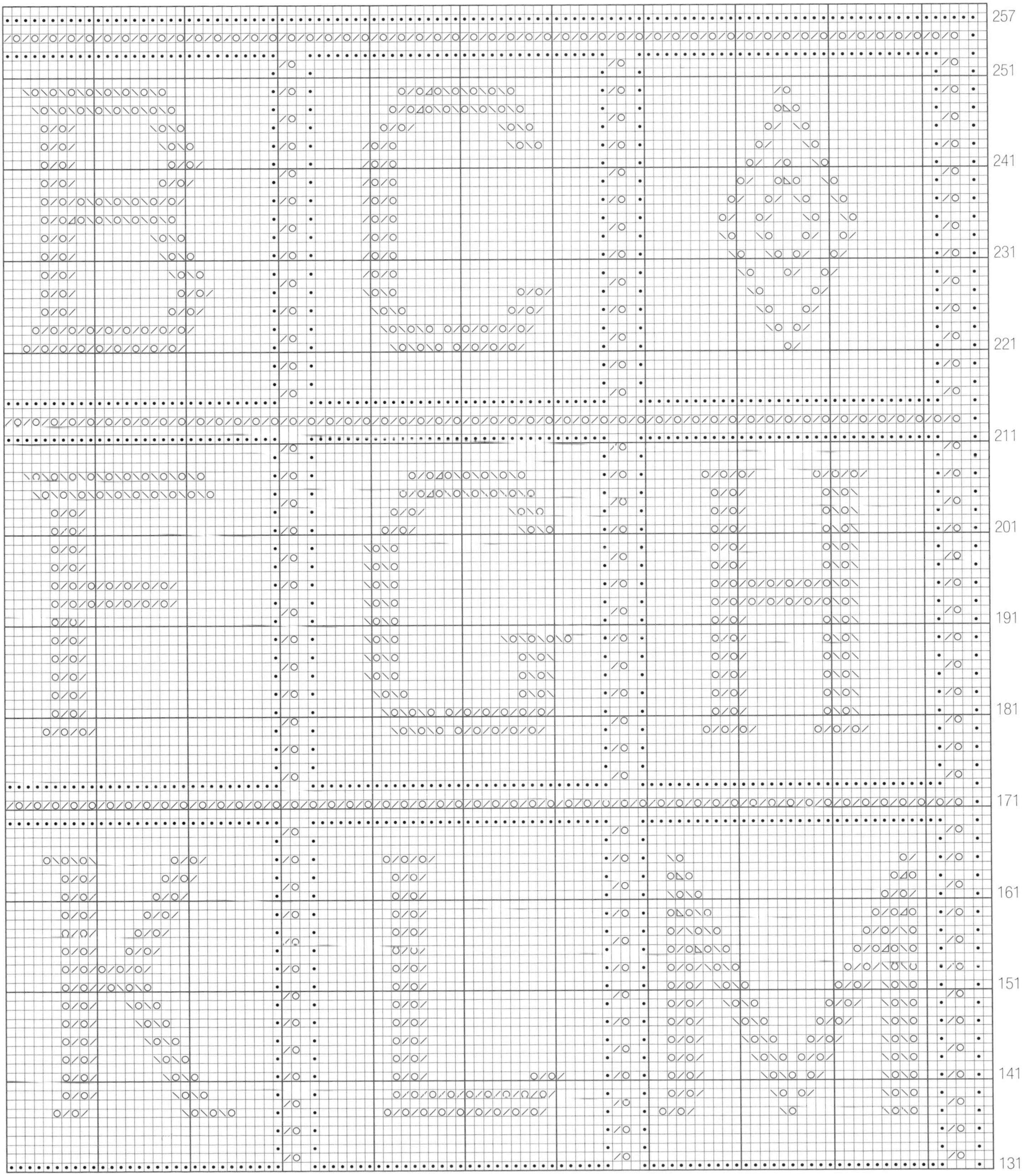

257
251
241
231
221
211
201
191
181
171
161
151
141
131

Note This chart starts on pages 120 and 121. Again, read
each chart row across this page and the page opposite.

the finishing touch

These simple garter stitch shoes are enhanced by introducing different elements to decorate the edge. As alternatives, you could pick up stitches around the edge and use the picot cast off from the sheep dress and shoes, embroider on simple lazy daisy stitches, or sew on tiny rose buds. I have used velvet piping, beads and fine ribbon, but you will find other ways to bring your own original style to this simple shoe pattern.

garter stitch shoes

Measurements

To fit ages   3-6   9-12   12-18   months

Materials

One 50g ball of Debbie Bliss baby cashmerino.
Pair of 2³⁄₄mm(US 2) knitting needles.
Beaded shoes: Approximately 250 small beads.
Ribbon shoes: 50cm/20in of narrow ribbon.
Piped edge shoes: 50cm/20in narrow velvet piping.

Tension

28 sts and 60 rows to 10cm/4in square over garter st (k every row) using 2³⁄₄mm(US 2) needles.

Abbreviations See page 7.

Note For safety reasons, make sure that beads are stitched on securely.

To make

With 2¾mm(US 2) needles, cast on 18(22:26) sts.

K 1 row.

Work in garter st and inc one st at each end of next and every foll alt row until there are 32(38:44) sts.

Dec one st at each end of next and every foll alt row until 18(22:26) sts rem.

Shape heel

Next row Cast on 7(8:9) sts, k these 7(8:9) sts, then k to end. 25(30:35) sts.

K 1 row.

Inc one st at end of next row and 5(6:7) foll alt rows. 31(37:43) sts.

K 1 row.

Next row Cast off 18(20:22) sts, k to last st, inc in last st. 14(18:22) sts.

K 14(18:22) rows.

Next row K2tog, k to end.

Next row Cast on 18(20:22) sts, k these 18(20:22) sts, then k to end. 31(37:43) sts.

Dec one st at beg of next and 5(6:7) foll alt rows. 25(30:35) sts.

K 1 row.

Cast off.

To make up

Join back heel seam. Join upper to sole all around easing in fullness at toes. Turn through to right side.

Beaded shoes – stitch small beads around the edge of each shoe.

Ribbon shoes – use a large eyed blunt needle to thread narrow ribbon around the edge of each shoe, beg and ending 5mm/¼in to either side of centre front. Tie in a bow.

Piped edge shoes – folding the cut ends under, stitch piping around the edge of each shoe.

Stockists of Debbie Bliss Yarn

See page 9 for descriptions of Debbie Bliss yarns. For stockists, please contact one of the following distributors:

UK Designer Yarns Ltd,
1 Tivoli Place, Ilkley, West Yorkshire LS29 8SU.
Tel: (01943) 604 123. Fax: (01943) 600 320.
tivolipl@aol.com

USA Knitting Fever Inc,
35 Debevoise Avenue, Roosevelt, NY 11575.
Tel: (516) 546-3600. Fax: (516) 546-6871.
www.knittingfever.com

Canada Diamond Yarns Ltd,
155 Martin Ross Avenue, Unit 3, Toronto, Ontario M3J 2L9.
Tel: (416) 736-6111. Fax: (416) 736-6112.
www.diamondyarn.com

Australia Sunspun Inspirations,
185 Canterbury Road, Canterbury, VIC 3126.
Tel: 03 9830 1609. Fax: 03 9888 5658.

Japan Eisaku Noro & Co Ltd,
55 Shimoda Ohibino Azaichou,
Ichinomita Aichi, 491 0105.
Tel: +81 52 203 5100. Fax: +81 52 203 5077.

Germany Klaus Koch,
Pontinusweg 7, D-50859 Köln.
Tel: +49 0170 5803 316. Fax: +49 02234 77573.
www.debbiebliss.de

France Elle Tricote,
8 Rue de Coq (Petite France), 67000 Strasbourg.
Tel: 0388 23 03 13. Fax: 0388 23 01 69.
www.elletricote.com

Belgium and Netherlands Pavan,
Koningin Astridlaan 78, Gent 9000
Tel: (09) 221 85 94 Email: pavan@pandora.be

Acknowledgements

This book would not have been possible without the contribution of the following people: The knitters, for their invaluable dedication and hard work: Dorothy Bayley, Cynthia Brent, Pat Church, Shirley Kennett, Penny Hill, Jaquie Dunt, Janet Kopinski, Maisie Lawrence, Frances Wallace. The creative and technical team: Jane Bunce for her tremendous practical and creative input and contributing the baby's kaftan. Jane Crowfoot, for her beautiful embroidery on the kaftan and shoes and the Fair Isle bag. Penny Hill for pattern compiling and providing an excellent knitter with her mother Pat Church, who also embroidered the jacket. Melody Griffiths for the lovely alphabet blanket and dressing gown. Rosy Tucker, for the cable and moss stitch jacket, and the topknot hat and socks. Sandra Lousada, not only for her beautiful photography, but also for her total commitment to this publication which went well beyond the call of duty! Sammie Bell, the stylist, for her perfect styling and creating the look. Rosy Tucker, for her expert pattern checking, and for being such a pleasure to work with. Denise Bates at Ebury, for initating the publications and her unfailing support throughout them. Maggie Town, for the design concept of the book. Sally Harding, the editor, for pulling it all together. The models – Charlie, Ella, Iris, Joey, Kieran, Kyran, Lavinia, Molly, Lauren, Lily, Tally, Somerset, Lea. Designer Yarns, for making my yarns possible. Brandon Mably, for being a good friend. Heather Jeeves, a great agent.